an **IISS** *strategic dossier*

ISR & THE GULF: AN ASSESSMENT

published by
The International Institute for Strategic Studies
ARUNDEL HOUSE | 6 TEMPLE PLACE | LONDON | WC2R 2PG | UK

an IISS strategic dossier

ISR & THE GULF: AN ASSESSMENT

The International Institute for Strategic Studies

ARUNDEL HOUSE | 6 TEMPLE PLACE | LONDON | WC2R 2PG | UK

DIRECTOR-GENERAL AND CHIEF EXECUTIVE **Dr John Chipman**
CONTRIBUTORS **Douglas Barrie, Nick Childs, Denis Fedutinov, Chris Pocock, David Roberts, Alan Warnes**
EDITORIAL **Alice Aveson, Alex Goodwin, Sara Hussain, Jill Lally, Jack May, Bao-Chau Pham**
DESIGN AND PRODUCTION **John Buck, Carolina Vargas, Kelly Verity**

This publication has been prepared by the Director-General and Chief Executive of the Institute and his staff. It incorporates commissioned contributions from recognised subject experts, which were reviewed by a range of experts in the field. The IISS would like to thank the various individuals who contributed their expertise to the compilation of this dossier. The responsibility for the contents is ours alone. The views expressed herein do not, and indeed cannot, represent a consensus of views among the worldwide membership of the Institute as a whole.

First published November 2019 by the International Institute for Strategic Studies.

© 2019 The International Institute for Strategic Studies

COVER IMAGES: Top: US Navy RQ-4 (Lt-Gen. Joseph Guastella, Commander, US Air Forces Central Command); bottom: failed Iranian rocket launch at the Imam Khomeini Space Center in Semnan, Iran, 29 August 2019 (Maxar Technologies/AFP); main: an image grab taken from a video handed out by Houthi rebels on 27 March 2018, showing what appears to be Houthi military forces launching a ballistic missile on 25 March reportedly from the capital Sanaa, Yemen (AFP Photo/HO/Huthi Rebels/Getty).

Printed and bound in the UK by Hobbs the Printers Ltd.

All rights reserved. No part of this book may be reprinted or reproduced or utilised in any form or by any electronic, mechanical, or other means, now known or hereafter invented, including photocopying and recording, or in any information storage or retrieval system, without permission in writing from the publishers.

British Library Cataloguing in Publication Data
A catalogue record for this book is available from the British Library

Library of Congress Cataloging in Publication Data
A catalog record for this book has been requested

ISBN 978-0-86079-219-2

About The International Institute for Strategic Studies

The International Institute for Strategic Studies is an independent centre for research, information and debate on the problems of conflict, however caused, that have, or potentially have, an important military content. The Staff of the Institute is international in composition and IISS work is international in its perspective and reach. The Institute is independent and it alone decides what activities to conduct. It owes no allegiance to any government, any group of governments or any political or other organisation. The IISS stresses rigorous fact-based research with a forward-looking policy orientation that can improve wider public understanding of international security problems and influence the development of sounder public policy, and more effective business decisions in the international arena.

Contents

Introduction   **5**

Chapter One
ISR: An Overview   **11**

Chapter Two
Regional Security Drivers   **29**

Chapter Three
Defence-industrial Aspirations and Challenges   **45**

Chapter Four
The Role of ISR in the Gulf   **61**

Chapter Five
Maritime ISR   **79**

Conclusion   **91**

Index   **97**

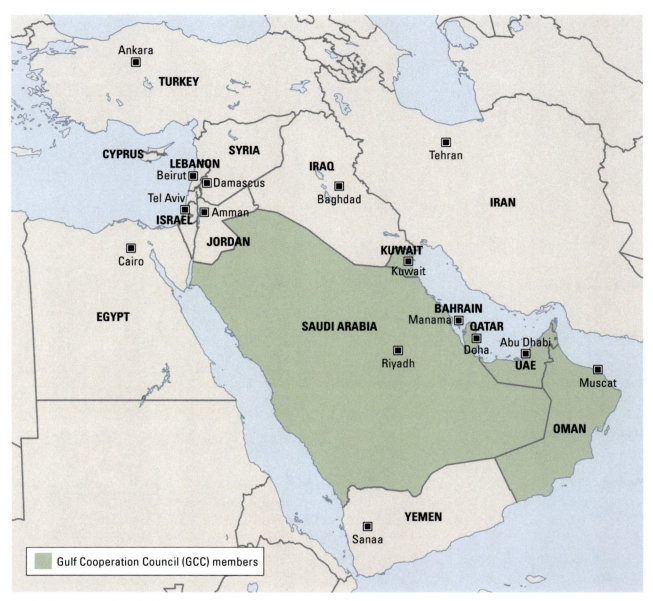

The Gulf Cooperation Council states and wider region

Introduction

This report considers the requirements for what is collectively termed intelligence, surveillance and reconnaissance (ISR) across the armed services of the Gulf Arab countries, and in the five domains: land, sea, air, space and cyber. It reviews how the six member states of the Gulf Cooperation Council (GCC) – Bahrain, Kuwait, Oman, Qatar, Saudi Arabia and the United Arab Emirates (UAE) – have so far attempted to meet national ISR requirements, and how these needs might be better fulfilled in the future. It also reviews how external security actors in the Gulf and wider Middle East region – including the United States and Russia – have used and continue to use national ISR capabilities to support regional security and foreign-policy goals.

As such, this report can be considered a companion work to the International Institute for Strategic Studies' (IISS) 2016 study *Missile-Defence Cooperation in the Gulf*,[1] which examined the threat that Iran's ballistic and cruise missiles pose to the GCC countries. Improving ISR capability is part of countering these continuing missile developments, while it will also aid broader regional security goals including greater stability for the Gulf. Since the publication of the 2016 dossier, Ansarullah – also known as the Houthis – has targeted Saudi Arabia using ballistic and cruise missiles.

Even in the narrow context of missile defence, ISR is a critical analytical and operational enabler. At the strategic level of decision-making, with the correct collectors – such as satellite systems – it can provide early warning of ballistic- or cruise-missile programme development, before it is a threat. At the operational level, ISR can support the identification of pre-prepared launch sites for mobile ballistic missiles and transporter erector launchers (TELs), as well as base and storage areas. Appropriate ISR platforms and sensors can also be used to help identify launches and to provide location and targeting data in

Houthi forces watching a ballistic-missile launch in Sanaa, Yemen, 27 March 2018

Introduction

near-real time to potentially enable a counter-strike before the TEL is relocated.

Missile defence is, however, only a small subset of the military and wider governmental security roles in which ISR plays a critical supporting role. ISR allows the military and government to see and understand the battlespace – remove it, and any military force is simply 'fighting blind'.

Behind the single framing question of this work – the requirements of ISR – are numerous multifaceted issues, including assessing what is understood by ISR. Furthermore, in order to consider future ISR requirements, the threats that the GCC now faces must be assessed: how these threats might evolve, and how ISR can be best employed to address them across all domains and across the spectrum from peace to war, as well as the many intermediate states captured in the concept of 'grey zone' activities, or tolerance warfare.[2]

ISR is known for its use in the tactical contact fight, where a ground unit has deployed an ISR asset, most likely a micro or mini uninhabited aerial vehicle (UAV), to see what is on the next street or over the next rise. However, another key characteristic of ISR is that among the more capable armed forces it is viewed fundamentally as a joint product. Such a product is one shared amongst a variety of interested parties, intra- or inter-service, or even at an alliance level.[3] This does not mean that any or all ISR platforms and capabilities must be held or operated at the joint level, rather that the information derived from ISR activity should be considered in terms of all-service exploitation. This may include national organisations or ministries other than defence. Additionally, in alliance or coalition environments the sharing of nationally acquired ISR has further benefits, providing that states are willing to distribute at least some of the information acquired through ISR activities. National-security caveats and release issues inevitably place restrictions on such information sharing, but within these boundaries the benefits are worth pursuing.

As with the missile-defence dossier, an exploration of the GCC states' ISR needs also raises the question of collective defence within the Arab Gulf nations, and the patchy nature of progress towards this.[4] The ability to share ISR-derived information as much as possible among some, though perhaps not all, GCC member states with regard to common threats should be an aim, particularly in addressing challenges such as Iran's ballistic- and cruise-missile arsenal, which continues to grow in size and capability.

Regional significance

The Gulf region remains important in terms of the global economy and for the security of Western states. However, the external security actors involved in the region also have wider defence and security interests, and the Gulf is competing for their attention with regions that are presenting growing security demands. The Middle East remains the world's largest crude-oil producing region, with almost all of the crude oil coming from the Gulf states.[5] Saudi Arabia was globally the second-largest producer after the US. Other producers along the Gulf coast include Bahrain, Iran, Iraq, Kuwait, Qatar and the UAE. As such, the Strait of Hormuz – the sea channel between Oman and Iran that links the Persian Gulf and the Gulf of Oman – remains of global economic significance. The strait is the most important conduit, and therefore choke point, for worldwide crude-oil supply, and disruption to this route would have unwelcome and potentially far-reaching effects on the global economy.[6] In the wake of 'minor' attacks on two oil tankers on 13 June 2019 in the Gulf of Oman, the crude-oil futures price increased, and the market was volatile.[7]

The vulnerability of the Strait of Hormuz to belligerent activity was exposed during the 1980–88 Iran–Iraq War, in the so-called 'Tanker War'.[8] This led to the involvement of the Soviet Union and the US in efforts to maintain the sea lanes through the strait. Hostilities between Iraq and Iran had only just ceased when the region was embroiled in further conflict when the former invaded Kuwait in 1990. This resulted in US-led military action forcing Iraq to withdraw, and the imposition of more than a decade of sanctions following the 1990–91 war.

In 2003, the US waged war on Iraq again, overthrowing president Saddam Hussein and removing the Ba'ath Party from power. While the military action was quickly concluded, the US and its allies were then involved in a decade-long counter-insurgency war that further weakened Iraq and opened it up to greater Iranian influence, while providing additional oxygen for Islamists. This culminated in the creation of al-Qaeda offshoot the Islamic State, also known as ISIS or ISIL, which established what it characterised as a 'caliphate' in territory crossing the border between Syria and Iraq. Iraqi state forces proved unable to defeat ISIS,[9] resulting in the US and its allies re-engaging in Iraq, and operating in Syria to dismantle the ISIS 'state'. The enduring significance of the region means that even when external actors attempt to reduce their presence they can be drawn back in.

The Gulf security environment

The GCC is arguably a *sui generis* 'security complex', involving internal tensions and external patrons, and a defence environment influenced by former colonial rulers. The United Kingdom's influence in the Gulf region began in the mid-eighteenth century, and the UK was the shaping power in the region almost until its departure in

US air power was brought to bear against ISIS in Deir ez-Zor province, Syria, in early March 2019

1971. By the end of that decade, the Gulf countries faced a deteriorating regional security picture.

A popular uprising ended the reign of the shah of Iran in 1979, but this broad front of opposition narrowed quickly to a militant Shia core. Islamism has been an increasing threat to the Gulf region ever since. The ideology of the Islamic republic and its leaders – such as Ayatollah Ruhollah Khomeini, who was a proselytising force for Shia Muslims – rejects the West and its influence in the region, irrespective of national boundaries.

A further attack on the influence of liberal Western ideals on the region came with the seizure of the Grand Mosque in Mecca by Sunni Islamists in November 1979. This was a challenge not just to the Saudi Arabians, but to all the rulers of the Arab Gulf states. The emerging Shia and Sunni militants, with an anti-Western agenda, increasingly found purchase among some of the region's wider population.

If the end of the 1970s was marked by the re-emergence of fundamentalist strains of Islam in the region, the 1980s was characterised by the 1980–88 Iran–Iraq War and its wider impact. There were attempts to destabilise the elites in Bahrain, Kuwait and Saudi Arabia. Although the actors were domestic, Tehran was rightly or wrongly assumed to be involved. An impact of the Iran–Iraq War was the transformation of the Iranian militias set up during the revolution into permanent forces, the Islamic Revolutionary Guard Corps (IRGC). These forces remain significant.

Regional responses to varied threats

The Arab Gulf nations set up the GCC in 1981 in response to the deteriorating security situation. All authority, however, remained vested in each of the member countries: the GCC had no power in its own right and it could not compel actions on the part of its members. These limiting factors have continued to inhibit the GCC's effectiveness and development since its founding. As highlighted by the IISS missile-defence dossier, the lack of progress in building collective defence in key areas is a result of the unwillingness of the Gulf Arab states' ruling elites to cede any sovereignty, even if there are clear defence and security benefits of doing so. The disparity in size among the GCC member states – Saudi Arabia is by far the largest in terms of area and population – is also a consideration. The UAE, however, is arguably the most militarily capable.

The hollowness of the GCC in terms of collective defence was exposed by Iraq's invasion of Kuwait in 1990. Rather than a unified response, the nations sought security from the US. The Peninsula Shield Force (PSF), the GCC's military arm established in 1982, was not collectively deployed during the crisis.

Introduction

The defeat of Iraq did not mark the start of a period of sustained regional stability. Iran remained a disruptive neighbour, and Iraq was as unpredictable as ever. The tragic events of 11 September 2001, however, resulted in responses that continue to roil the region to this day. The US-led invasion of Iraq in 2003, on the false premise that the regime continued to possess weapons of mass destruction, delivered a quick military victory. The lack of any credible reconstruction plan, however, meant that Iraq rapidly became a near-ungoverned space, and an environment that invited greater Iranian influence. This was a further unwelcome development for the GCC. In the years following the US-led invasion, Iran pursued a yet more assertive role.

The concerns of the GCC's ruling elites were compounded by the 2011 Arab Spring and, to varying degrees, pressure within their own countries for reform. In Bahrain, Shia protests led to the GCC deploying the PSF to support stability. Most of the GCC states considered that Tehran was actively supporting the protests in Bahrain, and the deployment was also intended to signal to the Iranian leadership that its meddling would be countered.

The GCC, the US and Russia

The US-orchestrated rapid military victories in Afghanistan and Iraq were followed not with the emergence of new and credible pro-Western power structures, but with bloody and prolonged counter-insurgency campaigns.[10]

As these wars dragged on, Washington's policy goals shifted from the lofty ambition of crafting 'democratic' governance in Afghanistan and Iraq to simply creating conditions in which it could draw down its forces and leave behind a semblance of stability. In broader defence and security terms, the US was becoming preoccupied with the emergence of China as a rival in what is now termed the Indo-Pacific. President Barack Obama's 'pivot' or 'rebalance' to Asia, coupled with a growing desire to get out of Iraq, raised concerns among the GCC states that the US was beginning to disengage from the region. While the GCC publicly supported the 2015 Joint Comprehensive Plan of Action with Iran to curtail its nuclear programme, the support was lukewarm at best. When US President Donald Trump unilaterally withdrew from the agreement in 2018, some in the GCC welcomed this development.[11]

Washington's wish to withdraw fully from Iraq was stymied by the emergence of ISIS, its declaration of a caliphate and the Iraqi Armed Forces' seeming inability to prevent it from seizing ever more territory. Beginning in late 2014, the US and its allies engaged in an air-led campaign to weaken ISIS. Meanwhile, Russia intervened in support of the Assad regime in Syria a year after the US began operations. Russia, ground forces from the IRGC and the rump of the Syrian Army rolled back not just ISIS, but all opposition forces. A second-order benefit for Moscow and Tehran was an increase in standing among some countries in the region, such as Egypt.

Increasing extroversion

While the GCC has often punched well below its collective weight,[12] some individual states have begun to adopt a more extrovert position on military action. The UAE took part in operations in Afghanistan, contributing a detachment of F-16 Block 60 aircraft, with a C-17 heavy transport aircraft providing the air bridge to support the mission. It was also involved in NATO air operations in Libya in 2011, along with Qatar. This growing confidence contributed to the decision to intervene militarily in Yemen in March 2015, in what the GCC leaders hoped would be a short operation. Yemen had grown increasingly unstable since 2011 and by 2014 civil war had broken out. The Houthis had seized the capital in September 2014, forcing the 'legitimate' government to leave. President Abd Rabbo Mansour Hadi went into exile in Saudi Arabia.

The Saudi Arabia-led coalition (Bahrain, Egypt, Jordan, Kuwait, Morocco, Qatar, Senegal, Sudan and the UAE) intervened to counter the rise of the Houthis, and what some saw as the growing influence of Iran in Yemen. The Royal Saudi Air Force (RSAF) and the UAE Air Force were the main contributors to the initial air campaign with RSAF *Typhoon* and *Tornado* and UAE F-16 Block 60 aircraft used for air-to-surface attacks. However, aspirations that the coalition could force a quick resolution were not met.

Air-campaign failings

The number of civilian deaths caused by Saudi Arabia-led coalition airstrikes rapidly became a political concern in the US and the UK, both of which provided combat aircraft and weapons to Saudi Arabia and the UAE. In response, in May 2016,[13] Saudi Arabia established the Joint Incidents Assessment Team (JIAT) to investigate incidents resulting in the deaths, or alleged deaths, of civilians. Coalition airstrikes in Yemen, however, continued to result in high-profile incidents in which large numbers of civilians were killed. In October 2016 at least 137 civilians died at a funeral in Sanaa,[14] while in August 2018 an airstrike on a bus killed 40 people, many of them children. The effectiveness, or otherwise, of the JIAT in identifying and addressing shortcomings remains a point of contention.

London and Washington's concern was compounded when Riyadh was implicated in the murder of Saudi Arabian journalist Jamal Khashoggi in October 2018.[15] In June 2019, the US Senate voted to block a weapons sale to

Introduction

UAE Air Force F-16 Block 60s, like these stationed in Jordan, have been used for airstrikes against ISIS and in its intervention in the Yemeni war

Saudi Arabia.[16] In the UK, a Court of Appeal ruling found that the government had not given enough consideration as to whether the proposed recipient of a weapons sale had breached international humanitarian law before approving an export licence.[17]

The US and the UK have since the early stages of the military engagement sent personnel to act in an advisory role in an attempt to ensure the efficacy of the air campaign, and to try to minimise the risk of civilian casualties. They have also provided intelligence support, likely to improve the targeting process.

Although Saudi Arabia and the UAE have acquired advanced combat aircraft and associated weaponry, they have relatively little combat experience, particularly in the challenging task of air-to-ground operations in a built-up environment. Such operations require a range of ISR platforms; the supporting analysis and exploitation infrastructure; and, most importantly, trained personnel able to make the best use of the product within the ISR process and throughout the command chain.

This dossier will consider what lessons the Yemen campaign may offer the GCC in terms of current ISR capabilities and possible future needs. It will also examine ISR in the wider context of the region, particularly with regard to Iran. And as demands grow on the US to provide greater ISR capabilities in other regions, primarily the Indo-Pacific but also Europe, it will also assess the extent to which the GCC should and can improve its own ISR capacity.

Scope of the dossier

This dossier is divided thematically, examining ISR, current capabilities and potential needs in the context of the Gulf region.

Chapter One considers what is generally understood by the phrase 'intelligence, surveillance and reconnaissance'. It examines the development of ISR in each of the five domains. It also reviews how the changing character of conflict, and the emergence once more of great-power rivalry, affects ISR. Finally, it assesses the considerable importance of ISR in the context of the Gulf region and the GCC countries.

Chapter Two describes the GCC member states' regional threat perceptions and their respective military drivers. It also examines the differences among the GCC states over Iran and how this colours their respective actions in the military realm, particularly with regard to ISR. In addition, this section considers the state threat of Iran.

Chapter Three considers regional defence-industrial aspirations concerning ISR, and the choices that Saudi Arabia and the UAE in particular have made in pursuing the acquisition of platforms and systems. It will also assess the influence that the multinational Missile Technology

Control Regime has had on regional choices, and the emergence of China as a supplier.

Chapter Four examines the use of ISR in the region in terms of the GCC and external actors. It also considers some of the significant ongoing acquisition programmes in the realm of ISR within the region, and the capabilities offered by such purchases. The region's approach to ISR UAVs is also featured.

Chapter Five reviews the maritime-security environment and the challenges of the Strait of Hormuz and beyond. It examines the US Navy's role in the region, and the demands that this role places on it, as well as other international actors. The growing capacity – albeit from a small base – of the GCC's navies is also considered.

In the Conclusion, this dossier assesses future options for the GCC states at the national and multilateral levels.

Notes

[1] IISS, *Missile-Defence Cooperation in the Gulf* (London: International Institute for Strategic Studies, 2016).

[2] IISS, 'Prospectives', *Strategic Survey 2018* (Abingdon: Routledge for the IISS, 2018), pp. 11–22.

[3] Curtis E. LeMay Center, 'US Air Force Doctrine, Annex 2-0 Global Integrated Intelligence, Surveillance & Reconnaissance Operations: Cross-domain Integration and Global Integrated ISR', 29 January 2015, https://www.doctrine.af.mil/Portals/61/documents/Annex_2-0/2-0-D05-ISR-Cross-Domain-INT.pdf.

[4] See Kenneth M. Pollack, *Armies of Sand: The Past, Present, and Future of Arab Military Effectiveness* (New York: Oxford University Press, 2019).

[5] US Energy Information Administration, 'What Countries Are the Top Producers and Consumers of Oil?', 22 April 2019, https://www.eia.gov/tools/faqs/faq.php?id=709&t=6.

[6] US Energy Information Administration, 'Today in Energy: The Strait of Hormuz is the World's Most Important Oil Transit Chokepoint', 20 June 2019, https://www.eia.gov/todayinenergy/detail.php?id=39932.

[7] Myra P. Saefong and Barbara Kollmeyer, 'Middle East Tensions Lift Oil, but Weaker Demand Prospects Push Prices Lower for the Week', MarketWatch, 14 June 2019, https://www.marketwatch.com/story/oil-prices-steady-as-market-keeps-watch-on-strait-of-hormuz-after-tanker-attacks-2019-06-14.

[8] David Crist, *The Twilight War: The Secret History of America's Thirty-Year Conflict with Iran* (New York: Penguin Books, 2013), p. 206.

[9] Pollack, *Armies of Sand*, pp. 494–5.

[10] See Theo Farrell, *Unwinnable: Britain's War in Afghanistan 2001–2014* (London: Vintage, 2018).

[11] 'UAE, Saudi Arabia and Bahrain welcome Trump's exit from Iran nuclear deal', *National*, 9 May 2018, https://www.thenational.ae/world/mena/uae-saudi-arabia-and-bahrain-welcome-trump-s-exit-from-iran-nuclear-deal-1.728557.

[12] Jeffrey Martini et al., 'The Outlook for Arab Gulf Cooperation', 2015, RAND Corporation, p. 9, https://www.rand.org/content/dam/rand/pubs/research_reports/RR1400/RR1429/RAND_RR1429.pdf.

[13] UK Foreign and Commonwealth Office, 'Freedom of Information Act 2000 Request Ref: FOI 0975-16', 12 December 2016, https://assets.publishing.service.gov.uk/government/uploads/system/uploads/attachment_data/file/582264/FOI_0975-16.pdf.

[14] UN High Commissioner for Human Rights, 'Situation of Human Rights in Yemen, Including Violations and Abuses Since September 2014', A/HRC/39/43, 17 August 2018, pp. 4, 6 and 8, https://www.ohchr.org/Documents/Countries/YE/A_HRC_39_43_EN.docx.

[15] US Department of State, 'Global Magnitsky Sanctions on Individuals Involved in the Killing of Jamal Khashoggi, Press Statement, Michael R. Pompeo, Secretary of State', 15 November 2018, https://www.state.gov/global-magnitsky-sanctions-on-individuals-involved-in-the-killing-of-jamal-khashoggi/.

[16] Catie Edmondson, 'Senate Votes to Block Trump's Arms Sales to Gulf Nations in Bipartisan Rebuke', *New York Times*, 20 June 2019, https://www.nytimes.com/2019/06/20/us/politics/saudi-arms-sales.html.

[17] See UK Court of Appeal Ruling, Case No: T3/2017/2079, 20 June 2019, https://www.judiciary.uk/wp-content/uploads/2019/06/CAAT-v-Secretary-of-State-and-Others-Open-12-June-2019.pdf.

Chapter One

ISR: An Overview

Next best to knowing what your military rivals are thinking is knowing where they are and perhaps even what they are saying. The attraction of such understanding spans from the tactical to the strategic, from the immediate to the long term, and across all domains: land, sea, air, space and, increasingly, cyber. The infrastructure and systems intended to provide such insight are often referred to collectively as intelligence, surveillance and reconnaissance (ISR).

The phrase 'forewarned is forearmed' can be traced back at least 600 years and reflects the essential importance of knowing your enemy. 'Taking the high ground' originally meant exactly that: the high ground offered commanders better situational awareness than that of the enemy. Attacking up hill was more demanding, not just physically. The quest for 'higher ground' – for a better view – is the enduring element of ISR. What is now called ISR is the mechanism that enables the military to cope with and at least partially see through what nineteenth-century military theorist Carl von Clausewitz labelled the 'fog of war' (*Nebel des Krieges* in German).

Balloons were being used for observation by the end of the 1700s. It was, however, with the arrival of powered flight and access to yet higher 'ground', and the adoption and exploitation of aircraft by the countries ensnared in the First World War, that the progenitor of what is now commonly known as ISR began to emerge. The Second World War served to fuel and accelerate the development of technologies for the reconnaissance and surveillance roles, as well as the intelligence structures to support the exploitation of what was gathered.

The military was exploring the use of cameras for reconnaissance to complement visual observation from fixed-wing aircraft by the 1900s. Handheld cameras were carried aloft for photo missions from the outset of the First World War in 1914. By the advent of the Second

Observation balloons, like this one in France, were in widespread use by the First World War

World War, wet-film cameras were fitted internally to military aircraft. The British *Spitfire* PR Mk III entered operation in 1940. This was the first photo-reconnaissance version of the *Spitfire* to be fielded in operationally relevant numbers. Interest in exploiting the radio-frequency element of the magnetic spectrum was also growing by the 1940s with advances in radar technology. A dedicated photo-reconnaissance variant of the US P-38 *Lightning*, the F-4, entered service in 1942.

Mechanical and analogue systems, however, only allowed for limited reconnaissance and surveillance. Image production and analysis was time-consuming, and cameras were comparatively large and limited by the amount of wet film they required. The film had to be returned to the ground for development, where a photograph interpreter analysed each frame.

The full impact of semiconductors and digital processors in the 1980s and 1990s offered a step change in performance and the ability to more rapidly acquire, analyse and exploit imagery or other data captured by increasingly capable sensors. As such, ISR is now a manifestation of what is often called the 'information age' – the digital infrastructure that underpins communication in modern societies. It is also increasingly central to how the United States, its allies and peer and near-peer rivals plan to fight wars.

Understanding the ISR acronym

While the words intelligence, surveillance and reconnaissance have long belonged in the military vocabulary, the three only came together as 'ISR' in the mid-1990s. The adoption of ISR into the military lexicon coincided with the language of the Revolution in Military Affairs. This phrase was an attempt to capture the impact of the 'information age' in the military realm.[1] As with much of the vocabulary associated with the military sphere, there are both narrow definitions and broader understandings of what ISR is. It has become shorthand for a range of capabilities and platforms that are growing in importance.

The US Department of Defense (DoD) *Dictionary of Military and Associated Terms* defines ISR as:

> 1. An integrated operations and intelligence activity that synchronizes and integrates the planning and operation of sensors, assets, and processing, exploitation, and dissemination systems in direct support of current and future operations. 2. The organizations or assets conducting such activities.[2]

The NATO definition is similar, though it replaces the word 'activity' with 'set of capabilities':

an integrated intelligence and operations set of capabilities, which synchronizes and integrates the planning and operations of all collection capabilities with processing, exploitation, and dissemination of the resulting information in direct support of planning, preparation, and execution of operations.[3]

In grappling with a definition of ISR, some have gone even further, arguing that implicit in the NATO definition is the assumption that ISR has become 'a word rather than an acronym'.[4] This dossier will adopt a wider and more flexible view of what ISR encompasses. It will consider ISR to cover the capability to collect data in one or more of the land, sea, air, space and cyber domains; the platforms and sensors used for these tasks; and the capacity to analyse the data captured to produce and disseminate intelligence in a timely fashion, be it at the tactical, operational or strategic levels of activity.

ISR and modern warfare

Since the end of the Cold War and the collapse of the Soviet Union, the US and its allies have been involved in a range of limited wars against states and, more often, non-state actors. Two wars have been waged against Iraq (in 1991 and 2003); an air campaign was waged against the Yugoslav government of Slobodan Milošević in 1999; military action removed the Taliban from power in Afghanistan in 2001; and an air operation indirectly led to the collapse of the Libyan regime of Muammar Gadhafi in 2011. Although the wars in Afghanistan and Iraq brought about regime change, the aftermath of both embroiled Washington and its allies in prolonged counter-insurgency campaigns with unsatisfactory outcomes. The emergence of the Islamic State, also known as ISIS or ISIL, forced the US and its allies to re-engage in Iraq and to become involved in the Syrian theatre, though only with the aim of destroying the caliphate.

From an air perspective, what was notable in all these wars was the ever-increasing use of air-launched precision-guided munitions, and the associated increase in accuracy. ISR is the less heralded but nonetheless critical enabler in this development.

Despite the rhetoric surrounding the Allies' strategic bombing campaign against Nazi Germany and imperial Japan during the Second World War, area attacks were required to have a realistic chance of having even a limited desired effect. In some missions in 1944, US bomber units were achieving a circular error probable (CEP – the radius of a circle within which half the weapons released will fall) of just over 1,000 metres.[5] By the time of the Kosovo War (1998–99), a CEP of less than 10 m was being achieved with the like of the Joint Direct Attack Munition (JDAM).

By the time of the Iraq War, more than two-thirds of the air-dropped weapons were guided, including these GBU-31 Joint Direct Attack Munitions

Accuracy requirements for the present and next generation of guided munitions have moved beyond a simple CEP, to a far higher percentage measurement of 'precision'.

Less than 10% of the air weaponry expended during the 1991 Gulf War was precision-guided;[6] by the Kosovo War that had risen to around 35%.[7] By 2003, the percentage of guided air-launched weaponry used in the Iraq War was 68%,[8] and in the 2011 intervention in Libya, effectively all the air-launched weapons used one or more forms of guidance.[9]

The age of the free-fall iron bomb, the staple of offensive air power for almost all of the twentieth century, appeared to be drawing to a close, at least for the West. Mass had been superseded by accuracy. The development of guided munitions obviated the need to drop large numbers of unguided bombs, the accuracy of which depended on the aircraft's navigational systems and, later, analogue computers to calculate the weapon-release point.

The success of an engagement, however, is dependent on the targeting information on which it is based, and ISR has a central role to play across all levels of campaign planning.

Permissive or otherwise

The US-led campaigns of the past three decades have mainly been carried out in what is termed a permissive air environment. While Iraq in 1991 had an integrated air-defence ground environment and a large number of Soviet-era surface-to-air missiles (SAMs), US and allied tactics rendered these mostly ineffective. Over the course of the war, the US and its allies lost 38 aircraft in combat, of which 13 were lost because of infrared-guided SAMs, ten as a result of radar-guided SAMs and nine due to anti-aircraft fire. Four were lost to unknown causes, one was shot down by an Iraqi Air Force MiG-25 *Foxbat*, and one further loss was ascribed to other 'direct enemy action'.[10]

Until the start of the US-led *Operation Inherent Resolve* against ISIS in Iraq and Syria in October 2014, the 1991 Gulf War had provided notionally the most capable air defences the US and its allies had faced. The US and its allies had to be cognisant of the Russian presence in Syria, and what was left of Syria's air defences, in their fight against ISIS. For the most part, the US and its partners were able to operate in relatively benign air environments, particularly where the focus was counter-insurgency activity. Here the threat was restricted to a very low altitude, coming from small-arms fire and rocket-propelled grenades; shoulder-fired infrared SAMs could also not be ignored. Airborne ISR was able to flourish in such a permissive environment, with little need to be overly concerned with the risk of being engaged. UAVs were increasingly exploited to provide persistent coverage of areas and individuals of interest. In this permissive environment, ISR UAV losses were more likely to be the result of operator or mechanical error than opponent activity.

The world is changing, however, and a permissive air environment can no longer be assumed. Washington's 2018 National Security Strategy says: 'Inter-state strategic competition, not terrorism, is now the primary concern in US national security.'[11] It adds:

> The central challenge to U.S. prosperity and security is the *re-emergence of long-term, strategic competition* by what the National Security Strategy classifies as revisionist powers. It is increasingly clear that China and Russia want to shape a world consistent with their authoritarian model – gaining veto authority over other nations' economic, diplomatic, and security decisions.[12]

Similar language can be found in the United Kingdom's 2018 defence review, the Modernising Defence Programme: 'After almost three decades of relative international stability, the world has now re-entered a period of persistent and intense state competition.'[13]

The threat of peer-on-peer or near-peer conflict, while still remote, is no longer unthinkable. In the context of ISR this has several drivers. One is the consideration that some ISR platforms will need to be able to operate and survive in a contested environment. This is true not only of crewed platforms but also of any highly capable multi-sensor UAVs where a low loss rate is required simply because of a lack of numbers driven by the cost of acquisition. Complementing the increasing requirement for surviv-able ISR air platforms, crewed and uninhabited, will be the greater exploration of low-cost UAVs that can be acquired in large numbers and fitted with comparatively inexpensive sensors. Here survivability will be based on mass, where a high loss rate will be accepted to provide mission-critical data. Longer-range sensors, which allow an ISR platform to be operated at greater stand-off range from the object or area of interest, also confer greater survivability.

The other driver is a renewed emphasis on 'strategic' ISR – redoubling efforts to build up an accurate intelligence picture of an adversary's current and potential capabilities in the medium and long term.

Conflict in the grey zone

ISR also has a role to play in what is sometimes called hybrid, grey-zone or tolerance warfare. This is where a rival state – or non-state actor – undertakes or is suspected of undertaking activities to undermine or destabilise a country, but the actions fall short of traditional military aggression. This raises issues of intent and attribution. Is the behaviour the precursor to a conventional attack? Is it probing activity? Is it intended only to keep the target state off balance? Is it some form of bargaining chip? Or could it be a false-flag operation?

A nation's ISR capabilities can help answer some of these questions. For instance, at the operational and strategic levels of surveillance, ISR could establish if there are any indicators of military activity associated with the preparation of a large-scale operation. If there are, then ISR capabilities could also establish if this is part of a

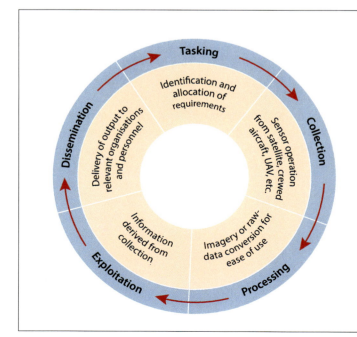

The intelligence cycle

While physical collectors such as crewed aircraft or UAVs are essential elements of ISR, the underlying end-to-end process needs to be fully managed and implemented to generate the best outcome.

The initial requirement is identified within the tasking process, and also considers which collector, or collectors, should be used to meet the specified request.

Collection is the physical process of gathering the data within the identified element of the electromagnetic spectrum, while processing manages the raw data to allow for ease of exploitation.

The latter generates information of intelligence value that should then be disseminated in a time-efficient manner to the relevant parties.

regular exercise cycle that has previously been observed, or if the activity is outside what would normally be seen.

Grey-zone activity also presents challenges regarding attribution. A state actor may not wish to be categorically identified as the source of malign behaviour. ISR capabilities can help provide direct or indirect material to support the identification of a perpetrator.

From data poor to data overload

In the military realm, the advent of digitisation has solved one problem, while in the process created another. Traditionally, ISR has been characterised by analysts picking over comparatively limited amounts of data. While most air- and space-borne ISR systems remain low density in terms of numbers, digital systems allow for the capture of a far greater quantity of data.

The combination of ever more powerful sensors, capable of seeing or sensing further and at greater resolution, is generating more and more data. This volume of material already presents a challenge for analysis, and the continuing profusion of emitters of interest will only prove a further challenge for some ISR systems.[14]

One approach to addressing the issue of the demands of data analysis is to implement at least part of the analysis on-board the platform used for collection. This can be done by human operators, but also select elements can be done by machine analysis, as is the case with some systems on the Lockheed Martin F-35 *Lightning* II.

Today the bandwidth demands of some ISR collectors when transmitting data, particularly live-streaming video, can compound the challenges of extracting actionable intelligence from ever-increasing amounts of data. Storage of large amounts of imagery in a structured fashion can also be a challenge. Overlay this with the sharing of intelligence in a coalition environment where partner nations are cleared for differing levels of access, and the scale of the challenge – as well as the promise – of advancing ISR capabilities is all too readily apparent.

ISR and the five domains

Given that ISR is so often a joint endeavour, it may seem arbitrary to consider each of the five domains individually. Yet each domain has specific characteristics and demands – some shared, others unique, with different levels of emphasis and need – that influence and shape the nature of ISR in each. All the domains can also lay claim to 'organic' capabilities, the ownership and direction of which is determined by the service that has primary responsibility for that domain. For instance, while air forces have 'ownership' of the air domain, some armies have organic air capabilities – fixed- and rotary-wing aircraft and uninhabited aerial vehicles (UAVs) – that are used in ISR roles.

The demarcation lines of responsibility are not always clear and need to be closely managed. While ISR is often branded as a joint asset or capability, simply saying so does not negate the challenge of inter-service rivalry and managing the allocation of what is likely to be a scarce resource. Demand will almost always outstrip availability regarding ISR systems. A land priority may appear less important to air-force personnel, or vice versa.

Land

War in the land domain can notionally occur somewhere on a spectrum that spans from purely attritional warfare to manoeuvre warfare. Simply put, at the state-on-state level, states can try to outstay their enemy by maintaining a larger army and a greater inventory, risking or accepting a higher rate of attrition of both personnel and equipment, until combat mass has its desired outcome. At the risk of oversimplification, this was certainly an element of the approach taken by the Soviet Union against Nazi Germany, when Moscow, after its near collapse following the initial devastation of *Operation Barbarossa* (1941), used its massive land area, industrial heft and large population as a source of conscription to generate the combat mass to help defeat the Nazi forces. One obvious problem with an attritional approach is the casualty rate: Soviet military losses during 1941–45 are now thought to have been in the order of nine million.[15]

The war in the West, by comparison, was often more manoeuvrist; direct attritional battles were not sought. Instead, efforts were made to exploit mobility to undermine the cohesion of the German army on the Western Front. The British-led *Operation Market Garden* in 1944 was a large-scale airborne drop of forces intended to outflank the Germans and seize bridges over the Rhine. If successful, it would have more rapidly opened Allied access to northern Germany.

Either approach – or more realistically a mix of the two of varying emphases – requires and benefits from elements of what today is described as ISR. In an attritional approach, 'strategic' ISR would be of great value if tasked with identifying the production capacities of military manufacturing plants. This was an insight the Soviet Union gained through the British Cambridge Spy Ring, for example. In the case of *Market Garden*, a failure of ISR contributed greatly to the outcome of the operation: the Allies failed to pick up the presence of German armour and elements of two tank divisions in the immediate area of the operation, and the presence of heavy armour proved decisive.

For as long as armies have fought, ISR has, in some shape or another, been part of military behaviour in the land domain. For centuries, the visual field provided the

Chapter One

The British Army used the *Desert Hawk* 3 mini-UAV in Afghanistan and Iraq, providing ground troops with organic ISR

primary sensor – initially unaided, and then supported by the benefits of magnification. Today, a far broader range of the electromagnetic spectrum can be accessed for ISR purposes. These fall into two main categories, sometimes called imagery intelligence and signals intelligence. The former is self-evident, while the latter is generally held to cover communications, electronic and telemetry intelligence.

ISR platforms and systems are generally held at the service level. At the army level, organic ISR systems can include fixed- and rotary-wing aircraft and UAVs, as well as signals-intelligence systems. In the case of the UK, for example, overall control of ISR capabilities during operations in Iraq and Afghanistan sat with the Air Component Commander (ACC). The UK ACC was able to call upon organic ISR assets from any of the UK armed forces deployed in theatre to fulfil tasking requests, and sometimes had to adjudicate between conflicting demands in the light of limited resources.

While within ground forces there has been an inevitable shift to increasingly exploit the air domain to provide ISR, ground-based systems have not been replaced completely. Rather, armies are continuing to find the right balance as technologies, systems and doctrines develop and change in response to perceived threats.

The British Army has a tradition of ground-based vehicle reconnaissance, including the Long Range Desert Group that operated successfully during the Second World War. The British Army continues to field and develop land-based ISR systems, although at various points in recent years the tensions and trade-offs between ground- and UAV-based systems have been apparent. This tension was at its most obvious with what was called the Tactical Reconnaissance Armoured Combat Equipment Requirement (TRACER). TRACER was a decade-long effort to acquire a successor to the *Scimitar* variant of the Combat Vehicle Reconnaissance (Tracked) that was abandoned in 2001.[16] In pursuing TRACER, the UK had joined with the US and its Future Scout and Cavalry System (FSCS) in putting together a demanding and ambitious requirement to meet land-component ISR needs. The vehicle was to be equipped with a highly capable sensor suite including electro-optical, infrared and radar underpinned by a digital combat-management system and a high-speed data bus. While the UK and the US did not ultimately pursue TRACER/FSCS, they have continued with other projects that are intended to meet at least some of these demands. For example, the British Army's *Ajax* programme – developing a family of combat vehicles – includes a reconnaissance variant that was due to begin trials in September 2019.

The impact of ISR can perhaps be seen most immediately in the land domain. The emergence of small hand-launched UAVs capable of transmitting real-time imagery provides ground forces with direct access to tactical ISR, without recourse necessarily to calling in support from a dedicated unit, or perhaps even another service branch, to conduct such ISR.

In the early years of this century, micro-air vehicles designed using digital components, microprocessors and compact sensors began to emerge in the land domain, providing previously unachievable levels of performance. The US and its allies in Iraq and Afghanistan pushed organic backpack (i.e., highly portable) ISR out into the field, as situational awareness for the 'boots on the ground' became ever more critical in order to minimise casualty rates, given public sensitivities in their home states.

Small UAVs from the likes of AeroVironment with its RQ-11 *Raven* and RQ-12 *Wasp*, and Lockheed Martin with its *Desert Hawk* family, found growing favour among ground forces. Handheld video receivers that allowed personnel to look at imagery in near-real time complemented such systems. British ground forces began operating early models of the *Desert Hawk* in 2003, purchased under what London terms an urgent operational requirement (UOR). This is used when there is a need to rapidly acquire a capability, most often off the shelf, while circumventing the more extended and rigorous proving trials the normal procurement process requires. The *Desert Hawk*s are operated by detachments of the Royal Regiment of Artillery – the first army unit to regularly operate UAVs intended for the artillery-spotting role. Examples of the smallest class of UAV brought into service included the *Black*

Hornet. This was ordered by the UK under a UOR in 2011, and is a palm-sized rotary nano UAV able to accommodate thermal and electro-optical cameras. It has a range of 2,000 m and an endurance of up to 25 minutes.

While US and allied ground forces have faced a variety of threats in combat operations since the turn of this century, until comparatively recently these threats have been limited in the air domain. Consequently, there was the underlying assumption that if something was overheard or in the vicinity then it must be friendly. This was particularly true of UAVs, where it was taken for granted that any in the vicinity posed no threat. This issue is compounded in part by the challenges of UAV recognition – telling yours from theirs – and the ability to then take countermeasures.[19] The absence of a UAV threat is no longer the case in the Gulf region, as the increasing use of a variety of UAVs by the likes of Iran and its partners attests.

Russia's extensive support of separatists in Ukraine in 2014–15 included the effective use of UAVs for ISR.[20] The Russian army used UAVs in support of a traditional emphasis on indirect fire (tube and rocket artillery). It also adopted a layered approach, with different types of UAVs used for target identification and the provision of target coordinates. The latter UAV would also be used to monitor the first artillery strikes and the imagery used for adjustments if required. This is the likely approach used

The UK Army in Iraq

British Army operations in Iraq have underscored the value of ISR in the land domain, while at the same time making apparent an initial lack of platforms as well as challenges in providing effective intelligence support for the UK-led Multi-National Division (South-East) (MND(SE)).[17] While persistent ISR was readily appreciated, there was a lack of UK resources at the local level within MND(SE) and sometimes an inability to effectively access joint ISR assets commanded and tasked at a higher level. In the case of the latter, this was in part because some of the ISR platforms, such as the *Nimrod* MR2, were also in demand for operations over Afghanistan. The MR2 was fitted with electro-optical sensors and had a video downlink.

While operating as part of a coalition force in MND(SE), the UK forces were not able to access UAV support from some of their partners in the region that did have tactical UAVs. Their priority, understandably, was to support their own forces. This experience served to further underscore the British Army's determination to secure and sustain its own organic tactical ISR systems. This has proved a prolonged and sometimes challenging process.

The fielding of the *Hermes* 450 medium-altitude long-endurance UAV and the smaller *Desert Hawk* was intended to provide such UAV support. The latter was used to contribute to force-protection tasks. The British Army began to operate the

Hermes 450, under a UOR, in support of the UK deployment in the south from July 2007. The *Hermes* 450 provided day/night electro-optical imagery and was operated by the 32nd Regiment Royal Artillery. The Royal Artillery had previously used the *Phoenix* UAV during the 2003 invasion of Iraq. The *Phoenix* was originally designed to support artillery spotting but had a chequered development. Almost half of the total of 75 UAVs were lost during its deployment in Iraq, but it did prove valuable.[18] Designed, however, for operations in Europe, the *Phoenix* air vehicle was underpowered to deal with the high daytime temperatures of the Iraqi summer. The *Hermes* 450 was also used in Afghanistan, where air attrition was also an issue. Between 2007 and 2012, 11 of the UAVs were lost, with operator error identified as the main cause. The *Hermes* 450 is also the basis for the British Army's *Watchkeeper* ISR UAV, which finally entered operational service in late 2018, if many years late.

A further challenge that became apparent during British involvement in Iraq was how to manage the dissemination of sensitive intelligence. Over-compartmentalisation and over-classification worked against the best use of the ISR material that was being gathered. An understandable desire to protect material at high levels of classification ran counter to providing information superiority. This was compounded when operating in a coalition.

Chapter One

Russia made effective use of UAVs in its broader support of Ukrainian separatists, including in the targeting of government-forces armour, such as this tank in Debaltseve, Ukraine, 2 March 2015

to devastating effect on several occasions, including the artillery attack on a Ukrainian armoured column near the village of Zelenopillya in July 2014, which resulted in the near destruction of two mechanised battalions in a matter of minutes. US Army analysis of the Russian use of UAVs in support of separatist forces in eastern Ukraine considers it to have been a game changer.

Maritime

While the land domain is characterised in part by the wide variety of physical terrain that ISR must accommodate, the maritime domain can, at its simplest, be categorised as either surface or sub-surface. If the physical environment, at least on the surface, is less challenging, the main issue is that of scale. Oceans make up more than two-thirds of the surface of the Earth, some 360m square kilometres (km^2). The Pacific Ocean alone is 155 million km^2. Even an aircraft-carrier task group can appear very small in terms of the open ocean. It is not just the surface environment that drives ISR requirements in the maritime domain. The sub-surface world provides some of the most challenging 'target' sets for maritime ISR, while also presenting an attractive environment from which to conduct ISR. That the US, Russia, the UK, France and now China consider the nuclear-powered ballistic-missile submarine (SSBN) to be the ultimate deterrent is testament to the challenges of locating, tracking and engaging a submerged submarine in the open ocean.

Although the environment is different, the same ISR cycle applies in the maritime realm: tasking, collection, processing, exploitation and dissemination hold as true for naval forces as they do for their land parallels. ISR in the maritime domain is a key element of core naval tasks such as anti-surface warfare, anti-submarine warfare (ASW) and maritime power projection as well as paramilitary roles such as counter-piracy operations, border patrol and the protection of exclusive economic zones, as well as search and rescue.

Such was the importance of maritime ISR during the confrontation between the US, its allies and the Soviet Union, that Moscow developed a dedicated class of satellites, deployed from the early 1970s, intended to locate and track US naval aircraft-carrier task groups and other surface combatants. There remains interest, yet unfulfilled, in using wake turbulence identified from orbit as a means of tracking submarines. Were this ever to become possible, and reliable, then the security of SSBNs as the most survivable of deterrents would be called into question.

While the phrase 'maritime domain awareness'[21] may be comparatively recent, what it represents is a fundamental tenet of war at sea. Closing with and engaging – as well as avoiding – the enemy has always required knowl-

Maritime-patrol aircraft, including this Japanese P-3C *Orion*, were part of the anti-piracy operation in the Gulf of Aden in 2012

edge of their location. The ability to see over the horizon, however, was only enabled by the arrival of powered flight in the early years of the last century. During the First World War, the belligerents were increasingly using aircraft for maritime reconnaissance.[22] From the outset, there has been a recognition that operational radius and endurance are important platform characteristics. Over the course of the twentieth century, platform development has been complemented by increasingly capable sensors, from optical to sonar and radar, infrared and electronic sensing. Such sensor fits are now standard on modern ships and submarines, as well as airborne maritime-ISR-capable aircraft, helicopters, UAVs (except sonar) and ultimately space-based sensor platforms.

As in the land domain, those in the maritime domain are faced with an ever-increasing amount of data and information, and the resulting challenges of timely analysis and dissemination. US government-funded think tank RAND noted in 2014 that 'as little as 5 percent of the data collected by ISR platforms actually reach the Navy analysts who need to see them'.[23]

Efforts to address these issues are ongoing within NATO and at the national level. NATO's Allied Command Transformation in 2016 set up a team to draft Alliance procedures for maritime ISR, with one aim being to better align the link between intelligence gathering and the joint ISR process. This work was in response to NATO's Military Committee Standardization Board, which had asked the Maritime Operations Working Group to explore an Allied Tactical Publication on maritime ISR.

Airborne maritime ISR platforms are now increasingly multi-role rather than simply intended for reconnaissance, anti-surface and anti-submarine warfare. As the costs of the aircraft and their mission systems have risen, this has increased pressure on acquisition numbers. The shift to multi-role platforms is an attempt to partly offset this problem. Irrespective of sensor ranges, any platform, however, can still only be in one place at a time. Among the NATO member states, the end of confrontation with the Soviet Union resulted in a reduced emphasis on anti-submarine operations, given the increasing absence of Russian submarine deployments during the 1990s and early 2000s. This change in the security environment also resulted in a shift towards multi-role aircraft and helicopters. As relations with Moscow have deteriorated and Russian submarine activity has begun to pick up, there is now renewed emphasis on ASW.

Counter-piracy, border control and marine-resource protection have also taken on greater importance in terms of maritime ISR, at the same time as there has been a return to the more traditional demands associated with peer-on-peer conflict. For instance, the use of the Mediterranean

Chapter One

Sea as a transit route for refugees and economic migrants occurred in parallel to renewed tensions between NATO and Russia, and increased deployment by the Russian Navy into the region.

Air

The air domain appears to be a – if not the – natural home of ISR. From tethered balloons first used in the eighteenth century to artillery spotting in the US Civil War in the 1860s; the 1960s SR-71 *Blackbird* high-altitude, high-speed reconnaissance aircraft; and systems such as the early 2000s RQ-170 and RQ-180 low-observable UAVs the following decade, the US has been a leader in the development of ISR in the air domain. Airborne ISR payloads began with optical systems but now also include radar, imaging and signals-intelligence payloads. Often, platforms will carry several sensor types that can be used to monitor the same area of interest or potential target.

The basic characteristics of air power – height, speed and reach – are particularly applicable to ISR. On the ground, with no obstruction, the visual horizon from eye level would be approximately 4.8 km; an elevation of 30.4 m (for example, a ship's mast) is 19.4 km; while at an altitude of 3.4 km the horizon is some 194 km. The attraction of gaining altitude for the purposes of ISR is therefore readily apparent. ISR is one of the four core roles of air power identified by the UK Ministry of Defence (MoD) in 2017: 'Intelligence, surveillance and reconnaissance informs the development of understanding across all environments.'[24] The other three roles are air mobility, attack and control of the air. ISR, besides being a role per se, also enables the other three.

Going faster, higher and further has been a design goal for nearly every generation of aircraft designer. The issue of endurance is pertinent to air vehicles in particular. Eventually fuel is exhausted, or the aircrew, or both. With ISR vehicles, relocating the pilot to a remote ground environment removes the limiting factor of human endurance, while the removal of aircrew-related systems, such as the cockpit and ejection seat, frees up volume and mass for additional fuel. This, however, still comes as a trade-off with speed. Long-endurance UAVs tend to be powered by turboprop engines, rather than turbofan engines. The turboprop-powered MQ-9 *Reaper/Predator* B has an endurance of around 40 hours, while the turbofan-powered *Predator* C *Avenger* has roughly half the endurance but a far higher air speed: 400 knots compared to 240 knots. The UK's *Zephyr* has been flown for up to 14 days; however, it is dependent on solar power, has a very lightweight airframe and a limited payload. Sometimes referred to as 'pseudo-satellites', the extent of their utility in the military realm remains to be seen.

The changing relationship between ISR and kinetic activity was captured by Lieutenant-General David A. Deptula; as US deputy chief of staff for ISR he gave the example of the mission that in 2006 killed Abu Musab al-Zarqawi, the leader of al-Qaeda in Iraq. Deptula said

> that operation consisted of over 600 hours of *Predator* time, followed by about ten minutes of F-16 time. The find, fix, track and target part of the equation in this case took far longer, and was much more complex than the engage part. So, are operations supported by intel, or is intel supported by operations?[25]

The MQ-9 is an example of a medium-altitude long-endurance UAV, and is used extensively in the region for tactical ISR and attack missions

Finding needles in a haystack

ISR in the air domain provides extraordinary utility and is critical to the use of kinetic attack. Nevertheless, it is neither infallible nor all-seeing and is subject to the same action–reaction behaviour from an opponent as any other military capability.

On the ground, mobility is now critical to survivability, with renewed emphasis on deception, decoys, emission control and remaining out of sensor view to counter airborne ISR, until required to move into the open for operational reasons. During the 1991 US-led war with Iraq, the Iraqis mounted a sustained campaign of *Scud* launches. These were not militarily effective, but were not intended to be; instead, they were used as a terror weapon and were an attempt to widen the war by luring Israel into the conflict. The US and its allies mounted a counter-campaign, so-called '*Scud*-hunting', which complicated but did not stop the missile firings. Post-war analysis cast doubt on the effectiveness of the air operation in destroying the mobile transporter erector launchers (TELs), but allied activity in the air, and the deployment of special forces on the ground, did curtail Iraqi freedom of operation.

Nearly 30 years later, Saudi Arabia and its allies are involved in the civil war in Yemen and face a similar geographical challenge. Ansarullah, the Houthi alliance they are fighting, has used artillery rockets, ballistic and cruise missiles and UAVs to strike at Saudi Arabia and the United Arab Emirates (UAE). Saudi Arabia and Yemen share a 1,458 km border, which is mostly sparsely inhabited. All the systems that the Houthis have deployed are mobile, and there is little open-source information on how many TELs, for instance, they have. This problem is compounded by Iran managing to supply and support the Houthis' UAV, ballistic- and cruise-missile inventories.

Ballistic- and cruise-missile launch vehicles are most vulnerable during the period immediately before and after the launch. This is not least because of the large infrared and visual signature a ballistic-missile launch has, although the solid booster of a ground-launched cruise missile is also significant, albeit for a shorter period. Identification, however, requires that an ISR sensor is pointed in the correct general area to pick up a launch, and that targeting and engagement can be executed before the launcher is relocated to a 'safe' area. A challenge for Saudi Arabia and its allies is that the Houthis can locate ballistic and cruise missiles in a large area, while still being able to launch against targets in the kingdom and the UAE. Some of the ballistic systems they use have a range of 800–1,000 km, while the cruise missiles may have a maximum range in excess of 1,000 km. In the case of the latter, however, firings appear to have been at considerably shorter engagement ranges.

Options to address the surveillance challenge could include high-altitude ISR platforms with long-range electro-optical and imaging infrared sensors, or a greater number of lower-altitude systems with a similar sensor suite. Near-real-time imagery of launches would have to be connected via data link to the appropriate command structure, to then allocate crewed combat aircraft to engage the TELs.

Iraqi *Scuds* proved a challenge to find during *Operation Desert Storm*; this reconnaissance-pod image shows a post-launch *Scud* site

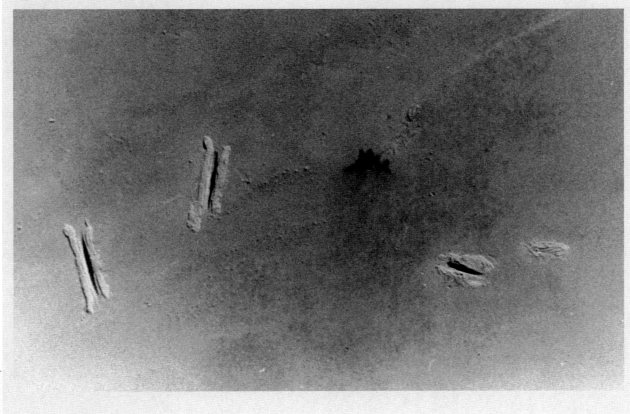

Deptula's final point may be rhetorical, but his example reflects two key shifts in air power: the increasing importance of ISR and the great improvements in weapons accuracy. Taken together, they provide modern air power with a conventional destructive capacity that requires far fewer platforms and weapons to deliver the same – or even greater – military effect than any previous generation. Both are underpinned by the same developments in technology, microprocessors and digitisation.

Those 600 hours of *Predator* flight time, however, occurred in a permissive air environment in which the surface-to-air threat was limited almost exclusively to small-arms fire. ISR platforms can be operated at leisure where the greatest concerns are either operator error or mechanical failure, rather than any surface-to-air threat. A permissive environment can no longer, however, be taken as a given. The re-emergence of great-power rivalry and the risk of peer-on-peer or near-peer war may further increase the threat in the air domain. The assumed permissive air environment is being superseded by a contested one, as ground-based threat systems continue to improve and proliferate and more capable combat aircraft enter countries' inventories. Potential rivals have also recognised the importance of ISR and, along with developing their own capabilities, are increasingly looking to passive and active countermeasures to degrade any opponent's ISR advantage.

UAV losses from surface-to-air engagements have increased in recent years, with man-portable and – on occasion – medium-range SAMs being used. This vulnerability was underscored on 20 June 2019 when an Iranian medium-range SAM shot down a US Navy Broad Area Maritime Surveillance Demonstrator (RQ-4A Block 10) over the Strait of Hormuz while it was being used to conduct an ISR mission. Tehran claimed that it was being flown inside its national airspace, while Washington maintained that it was in international airspace.[26]

Survivability in a high-threat environment is again a consideration for air-domain ISR platform developers and operators. A range of design and operational approaches are being considered or already being introduced to try to mitigate the worst of the risks. Platform attrition rates, however, are only likely to increase, and ISR will have to be fought for rather than taken for granted. At the exquisite end of the air-platform spectrum, the US is working on very low-observable ISR designs capable of being operated and surviving in a highly contested environment. It is also exploring the applicability of the use of large numbers of low-cost and comparatively simple sensor platforms where high attrition rates could be accepted, while still meeting ISR needs. One approach being considered to try to mitigate this risk is the modification of how some of the current generation of systems and UAVs are operated.

Space

Orbital systems provide the capacity to overfly an area of interest unimpeded by the risks of penetrating another nation's airspace, or the sensor limits imposed by remaining in international airspace skirting an area of interest. Space-based ISR can provide electro-optical and radar imagery and signals and communications intelligence for a broad range of military applications.

The US launched *Corona* – its first optical-reconnaissance satellite – in 1959, with a first successful mission in August 1960, while its first electronic-intelligence satellite, *Grab*, was launched in 1960. The Soviet Union launched its first *Zenit-2* reconnaissance satellite at the end of 1961. The first successful *Corona* mission, known at the time publicly as *Discoverer* 14, provided photo imagery of 3.8 million km² of the Soviet Union, including photos of 64 airfields, and gave the location of 26 SAM sites.[27] The *Corona* recovery capsule was 'hooked' during its parachute descent by a modified US Air Force (USAF) aircraft to allow the wet film to be recovered and developed.

Although early reconnaissance satellites were of huge value, they did not provide real-time imagery. Optical cameras are used to capture images of swaths of the Earth's surface. Russia's *Zenit-2* took 60×60 km images with a resolution of 10–15 m, while the first *Corona* camera had a resolution of 11–12 m; during the project the resolution was improved to around 2.9 m.

Even if the lure of space-based ISR were irresistible, the costs of entry were until recently prohibitively expensive. A launch vehicle and launch infrastructure were required, while the satellite buses and payloads were very expensive to develop and required support from an advanced scientific and industrial base. Until the 1980s, wet-film imagery had to be physically recovered to Earth; a photo-reconnaissance satellite's operational life was therefore limited by the quantity of wet film and re-entry vehicles it could carry. Begun in 1966, the US 1970s KH-9 *Hexagon* reconnaissance satellite had four re-entry vehicles. The *Hexagon*'s two cameras provided stereo imagery that allowed objects' heights to be determined. According to declassified performance figures, the KH-9 cameras provided up to 0.6–1 m resolution imagery with a 370 nautical mile swath. This meant that objects as small as 0.6 m in length could be identified on the picture. The satellite normally remained in orbit for up to 124 days. It was sometimes used to cue the KH-8 *Gambit* reconnaissance satellite. If recovered imagery showed an area of interest, then a *Gambit* could be launched to provide higher-resolution spot imagery. *Gambit* satellites

The size of a single-decker bus, the US *Hexagon* was a 1970s state-of-the-art reconnaissance satellite

remained in orbit for a far shorter period, only up to six days. Details of the *Hexagon* programme were only partly declassified in 2011[28] with, for instance, the imagery-resolution figures believed to be even better than those made public.

The extraordinary technical challenges of projects such as *Hexagon* meant that space-based ISR remained an exclusive club until the technological development of the past three decades increasingly opened it up to others. These included the emergence of a commercial satellite-launch market, much lower-cost satellites and the impact of digitisation. The USAF's National Air and Space Intelligence Center (NASIC) suggests that 45 nations now have ISR or remote-sensing satellites in service. Even if a country does not want its own space-based ISR capability, numerous commercial imagery providers offer resolutions down to 0.3 m.

Electro-optical sensors now include multispectral and, more recently, hyperspectral systems. The former can produce imagery while operating across 3–10 bands (i.e., discrete ranges of wavelengths) within the visible-light and infrared spectra; the latter can capture spectral data across hundreds of narrower bands. One advantage of a hyperspectral system is that it allows the detection of small spectral differences that would not be apparent using only a multispectral sensor. This has military utility in, for example, better identifying vehicles that are camouflaged or hidden by foliage. Imagery-tasked satellites are normally flown in either low or medium Earth orbit (LEO/MEO). LEO can provide better resolution and a quicker revisit rate than a comparable system in MEO. Advantages of MEO include greater coverage with fewer satellites.

The KH-9 *Hexagon* weighed just under 15,000 kg. In 2005, the UK MoD launched *TopSat* (Tactical Operational Satellite). At around 2.5 m, the resolution was not quite as high as that of the KH-9, but it only weighed 114 kg, less than one-hundredth of the 1970s US system. Small satellites are now capable of providing multispectral imagery of considerable military utility at a fraction of the development and launch costs of a traditional system, with the small satellite category generally held to cover systems up to 500 kg. In 2018, the UK MoD followed up *TopSat* with *Carbonite*-2. This provides around 1 m resolution imagery and video imagery in a 6 km swath.

The UK MoD has long enjoyed highly privileged access to US satellite imagery and continues to do so. However, its interest in small satellites is in part the recognition that, irrespective of the closeness of the relationship with Washington, US military priorities would inevitably come first. Exploring the development of a sovereign capacity based on small satellites provides a

Chapter One

> ### Action and reaction in the space domain
>
> One considerable attraction of space-based ISR has been the platform's near invulnerability when compared to crewed aircraft or UAVs. While both the US and the Soviet Union worked on anti-satellite systems at the height of the Cold War, the probability of overall system survivability remained relatively high.
>
> As space-based systems have grown in utility and as great-power competition has re-emerged, counter-space research and development has received renewed emphasis. China, Russia and the US are all carrying out research and development into soft- and hard-kill systems to defeat ISR satellites. All three have the capacity to engage satellites in LEO using ground-based interceptors, while Russia at least appears to be testing an air-launched anti-satellite (ASAT) weapon.[30] Both the US and the Soviet Union carried out ASAT tests in the 1980s. The Russian system now thought to be in-test may well build on the 1980s *Contact* 30P6 system, which used a modified MiG-31 *Foxhound*, the MiG-31D, as the launch platform for a large missile. Imagery of a modified MiG-31 with a large missile carried on the centre line appeared in 2019 on Russian social media. Russian President Vladimir Putin was also shown a MiG-31K fitted with a large missile during a visit to an air-force test centre in May 2019. Accompanying Russian journalists were not allowed to view what Putin was shown.
>
> India became the fourth country to test a hard-kill capability against a satellite in LEO in March 2019, when it used a PDV-Mk II to carry out the intercept. The US Defense Intelligence Agency assesses that China already has an operational ASAT weapon, and suggests that Russia will deploy a ground-based mobile system capable of destroying satellites in LEO 'within the next several years'.[31]
>
> Alongside ground-based hard-kill systems, some states may also be pursuing on-orbit threat systems. Russia and the US, for instance, appear to be exploring the possibilities for such capabilities. Russia has an 'inspection satellite' that can approach another satellite for repair purposes, which could arguably also be used for a more malign intent. Meanwhile, the US X-37B orbital test vehicle has also provoked speculation as to some of the roles this system might be able to fulfil.[32]
>
> If used, hard-kill capabilities are liable to be construed as an act of war by the party targeted. Moscow and Beijing, and possibly Washington, are also pursuing soft-kill options. Laser systems are capable of 'blinding' a satellite's electro-optical sensors. Depending on the power of the laser and the dwell time of the system on the sensor aperture, the effect could be transient or permanent. One countermeasure is to provide the sensor aperture with the ability to detect if it is being targeted by a laser and to quickly deploy a protective cover. If, however, the intent of the attack is simply to stop imagery of an area being captured, then the desired effect will already have been achieved.
>
> Electronic countermeasures such as jamming could also be employed in an attempt to disrupt either the satellite downlink or uplink.

route to an affordable and responsive space-based ISR capability at the national level.[29]

As suggested by the NASIC figure, the emergence of small satellites suitable for ISR makes such capabilities accessible to many countries that would previously not have been able to afford such a system. Ensuring access to space, rather than being able to afford to develop and acquire the orbital sensor platform, is now a forcing factor. Launch platforms can be booked for months in advance. This is in part why there is now renewed interest in developing lower-cost launch systems, such as reusable rockets, or single-stage-to-orbit launch vehicles.

Cyber

The US DoD describes cyberspace as: 'the domain within the information environment that consists of the interdependent network of information-technology infrastructures and resident data. It includes the internet,

Satellite imagery resolution

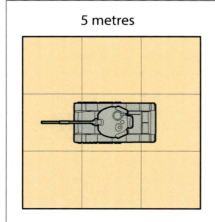
5 metres

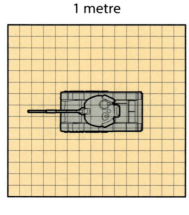
1 metre

Military-applicable satellite imagery now tends to be either high or very high resolution. The former provides spatial resolution of at least 5 metres, while the latter provides resolution of 1 m or less. Resolution can be considered as representing the size of a single pixel, so a 5 m resolution image would clearly show only objects of 5 m or more, while a 1 m resolution would show objects of 1 m or greater. The higher the resolution, the greater the detail of the available imagery.

telecommunications networks, computer systems, and embedded processors and controllers.'[33] As such, it is an essential environment for ISR exploitation.

Cyberspace is distinct from the other four domains in several ways. It is an information domain rather than a physical realm, although it has physical elements; it is an enabler acting as a conduit and repository that allows the military to optimise use of the other four domains; and, most distinctly, it is a human construct. The other four domains have required humans to develop technologies to move across and within them, but the cyber domain is a creation of human enterprise. Cyberspace, however, has dependencies in the four physical domains that facilitate its use, and fundamentally allow it to exist.

All that said, the cyber domain shares with the other four some basic characteristics that provide it with great utility in terms of ISR. It has efficacy across the spectrum of state-to-state relations from peace to war, and in the grey zone where 'hostile' activity in the information realm can be prevalent and below the threshold of overt military action. And like in the other domains, the best use of the data that can be acquired requires the appropriate organisational structures that can operate at the 'speed of relevance' to provide actionable information to those who need it or can exploit it for military advantage. This can be at the tactical, operational or strategic level, while 'relevance' may be a matter of minutes, hours, days or even an indefinite period at the strategic level. ISR in the cyber domain is able to support long-term policymaking in the defence realm, providing a 'deep look' into states of interest, which air, land and maritime ISR are less able to provide. Cyberspace, like physical space, offers global reach.

ISR in the cyber realm supports both offensive and defensive cyber operations, including as a means of exploitation for both; it also acts as a tasking mechanism for the former. Offensive cyber operations include the covert acquisition of intelligence information, and of data that can be exploited for wider intelligence purposes. The requirements-development chain for such activity may have been initiated by reconnaissance operations in the information realm, or by a requirement raised by ISR collectors in one of the physical realms. Cyber-reconnaissance operations include the covert and open exploration of the digital information domain to identify and collect information or activity that has utility for defence and security. In turn, such activity may result in surveillance tasking in the digital realm, either covert or overt. Such surveillance may be focused on an actor of interest's presence and use of the domain. The actor could range from an individual to a non-state organisation to a state.

ISR also has a clear role to play in defensive cyber operations. Offensive and defensive operations in the cyber realm are not discrete; they can be closely interrelated. Offensive ISR operations that shed light on a rival's information-domain operations may trigger defensive activities. Reconnaissance of national cyber capacity at the state and civil levels, in the case of the latter where legally acceptable (at least notionally), can be carried out to look for covert foreign activity, state or non-state. State-level actors pose the greater threat given the level of investment and capability that can be brought to bear. This, however, is not to dismiss the threat posed by non-state actors and even individuals.

Once an intrusion or active threat has been identified due to reconnaissance, then a decision may be taken to carry out surveillance. This may be prompted by interest in building an intelligence picture of the threat activities, possible aims and intentions, and to scope the level of damage that may have already resulted. Immediate denial of access is the alternative course of action to attempt to end the unapproved activity.

The nature of cyberspace poses difficulties in attribution given the diffuse and multilayered nature of the information environment. The US DoD notes: 'Due to the characteristics of the physical network, logical network, and cyber-persona layers of cyberspace, attribution of malicious cyberspace activity to a specific person, criminal organization, non-state threat, or even a responsible nation-state can be exceptionally difficult.'[34] State actors can mask activities through remote operations and the use of proxies, both physical and in terms of information systems, which can leave the target state struggling to cope not only with the effect of the intrusion, but also to identify the perpetrator.

ISR offers both direct and indirect support in meeting the challenge of attribution. It can identify malign or unauthorised activity, and can be used to begin to track back to the source of an attack or breach. Broader ISR activity in the information domain can also help build a picture of potential state and non-state threats; the level of threat each presents; and the kinds of capabilities they could use in offensive operations. ISR in the information domain can also support the verification, or otherwise, of a range of defence-related treaties and accords.

ISR in the cyber domain should fundamentally be a joint endeavour since, as with the other domains, exploitation is key to effectiveness. This does not mean that all information-domain ISR operations are joint service, since each will have its own needs and emphasis. Rather, it requires that training within the services emphasises the inherently joint nature of the activity, and that single-service activities are nested within a broader recognition of the potential multi-service utility of any ISR activity.

Chapter One

ISR and the Gulf region

The Gulf region and its near neighbourhood have faced and continue to face a range of security problems, both external and internal. The wider Middle East region remains volatile: the Syrian civil war has yet to end, though the regime of Bashar al-Assad has so far managed to survive as a result of the direct intervention of Russia and Iran; Egypt is contending with ISIS-associated groups in Sinai; and Libya is a failing state. The Gulf Cooperation Council (GCC) countries, led by Saudi Arabia and the UAE, have struggled to bring to a successful conclusion what was intended to be a short intervention in the civil war in Yemen.

The regional importance of ISR – tactical, operational and strategic – can be gauged by the extent to which the US continues to deploy key capabilities in support of both its operations and its regional allies. *Operation Inherent Resolve* was set up to counter ISIS in Iraq and Syria, and the territory it claimed as a caliphate in a region that spanned the Iraq–Syria border. The air mission was central to the operation, according to the Combined Joint Task Force–Operation Inherent Resolve: 'Deliberate and dynamic precision airstrikes targeted ISIS economic infrastructure significantly degrading its ability to govern. More than 15,000 coalition airstrikes destroyed enemy military capabilities and provided freedom of maneuver to regional security and partner forces.'[35]

These precision airstrikes were enabled by the United States' array of ISR systems and the exploitation of the intelligence, analysis and command-and-control architecture that enables the transformation of raw data into actionable intelligence. The two types of airstrikes mentioned, 'deliberate' and 'dynamic', are each underpinned by ISR, but in differing ways. Deliberate strikes are part of the wider air-tasking cycle; in the USAF this produces a 24-hour activity schedule including pre-planned targets. Dynamic targeting, meanwhile, is based on far shorter timelines where the target is not part of the pre-planned air-tasking cycle. At its simplest, visual identification by air or ground forces of a potential target of interest can begin a dynamic targeting cycle. Airborne ISR platforms, crewed or uninhabited, can also supply the initial data that results in a dynamic targeting event, or can be tasked quickly with providing supporting imagery, for example to confirm a target and to enable its engagement.

The USAF's 99th Expeditionary Reconnaissance Squadron is part of the 380th Air Expeditionary Wing, which has been at Al Dhafra in the UAE since 2002. The squadron operates the Lockheed Martin U-2 crewed aircraft and the Northrop Grumman RQ-4 *Global Hawk* high-altitude long-endurance UAV. Both platforms are equipped with multi-mode radar, electro-optical and infrared sensors capable of providing high-resolution imagery at extended ranges. The UAV workhorse in theatre for tactical ISR and for target engagement is the General Atomics MQ-9 *Reaper*, the successor to the MQ-1 *Predator*. The Lockheed Martin RQ-170 *Sentinel* UAV has also been deployed in support of regional activities, although the air force has made little about it public. Imagery of the air vehicle, however, shows a flying-wing design, with radar-signature management features. One was lost over Iran in December 2011, resulting in its recovery by Tehran.

With the exception of the MQ-9, of which the air force now has more than 250, the rest of the above ISR platforms are so-called 'low-density, high-demand' systems. This is in part a function of cost, and in part a function of the ever-increasing requirement for ISR.

Notes

1 Norman C. Davis, 'An Information-based Revolution in Military Affairs', in John Arquilla and David Ronfeldt (eds.), *In Athena's Camp: Preparing for Conflict in the Information Age* (Santa Monica, CA: RAND Corporation, 1997), pp. 85–6, https://www.rand.org/content/dam/rand/pubs/monograph_reports/MR880/MR880.ch4.pdf.

2 US Department of Defense, DOD Dictionary of Military and Associated Terms, July 2019, p. 113, https://www.jcs.mil/Portals/36/Documents/Doctrine/pubs/dictionary.pdf.

3 NATO Standardization Office, 'NATO Standard AJP-3.3 Allied Joint Doctrine for Air and Space Operations', Edition B Version 1, April 2016, pp. 1–15, https://assets.publishing.service.gov.uk/government/uploads/system/uploads/attachment_data/file/624137/doctrine_nato_air_space_ops_ajp_3_3.pdf.

4 Air Power Development Centre, 'What is ISR? Clarifying ISR and ISTAR in Air Power Terms', *Pathfinder: Air Power Development Centre Bulletin*, no. 117, August 2009, http://airpower.airforce.gov.au/APDC/media/PDF-Files/Pathfinder/PF117-What-is-ISR-Clarifying-ISR-and-ISTAR-in-Air-Power-Terms.pdf.

5 Jill A. Long, 'The Problem with "Precision": Managing Expectations for Air Power', United States Army War College Strategy Research Project, 2012, p. 8, https://apps.dtic.mil/dtic/tr/fulltext/u2/a589415.pdf.

6 See Richard P. Hallion, 'Precision Guided Munitions and the New Era of Warfare', RAAF Air Power Studies Centre Working Papers no. 53, 1995, https://fas.org/man/dod-101/sys/smart/docs/paper53.htm.

7 W.J. Fenrick, 'Targeting and Proportionality During the NATO Bombing Campaign Against Yugoslavia', *European Journal of International Law*, vol. 12, no. 3, 2001, p. 489, http://www.ejil.org/pdfs/12/3/1529.pdf.

8 Carl Conetta, 'Catastrophic Interdiction: Air Power and the Collapse of the Iraqi Field Army in the 2003 War', Project on Defense Alternatives Briefing Memo no. 30, 26 September 2003, p. 2, https://www.comw.org/pda/fulltext/0309bm30.pdf.

9 Karl P. Mueller (ed.), 'Precision and Purpose: Airpower in the Libyan Civil War', RAND Corporation, 2015, p. 4, https://www.rand.org/content/dam/rand/pubs/research_reports/RR600/RR676/RAND_RR676.pdf.

10 US Defense Technical Information Center, 'Gulf War Air Power Survey, Volume V: A Statistical Compendium and Chronology', 1993, p. 641, https://media.defense.gov/2010/Sep/27/2001329816/-1/-1/0/AFD-100927-065.pdf.

11 US Department of Defense, 'Summary of the 2018 National Defense Strategy of the United States of America', 2018, p. 1, https://dod.defense.gov/Portals/1/Documents/pubs/2018-National-Defense-Strategy-Summary.pdf.

12 Ibid., p. 2.

13 UK Ministry of Defence, 'Mobilising, Modernising & Transforming Defence: A Report on the Modernising Defence Programme', December 2018, p. 12, https://assets.publishing.service.gov.uk/government/uploads/system/uploads/attachment_data/file/765879/ModernisingDefenceProgramme_report_2018_FINAL.pdf.

14 See UK Ministry of Defence, 'Global Strategic Trends: The Future Starts Today', Sixth Edition, p. 144, https://assets.publishing.service.gov.uk/government/uploads/system/uploads/attachment_data/file/771309/Global_Strategic_Trends_-_The_Future_Starts_Today.pdf.

15 John Barber and Mark Harrison, 'Patriotic War, 1941–45', in Ronald Grigor Suny (ed.), *The Cambridge History of Russia, Volume III The Twentieth Century* (Cambridge: Cambridge University Press, 2006), p. 225, http://www.cultorweb.com/eBooks/Storia/Cambridge%20Hist%20Russia/THE%20CAMBRIDGE%20HISTORY%20OF%20RUSSIA,%20Volume%20III%20-%20The%20Twentieth%20Century.pdf.

16 'US, UK will Cancel Future Scout Vehicle Project', *Jane's Defence Weekly*, 19 October 2001, https://janes.ihs.com/Janes/Display/jdw03560-jdw-2001.

17 The Report of the Iraq Inquiry, Section 14.1 Military Equipment (Post-Conflict), 6 July 2016, p. 145, https://webarchive.national-archives.gov.uk/20160708115334/http://www.iraqinquiry.org.uk/media/246636/the-report-of-the-iraq-inquiry_section-141.pdf.

18 Ibid., p. 147.

19 Jeffrey Lamport and Anthony Scotto, 'Countering the UAS Threat from a Joint Perspective', p. 2, https://www.eglin.af.mil/Portals/56/documents/JDAT%20docs/Countering%20UAS%20Threats%20from%20a%20Joint%20Perspective%20(JDAT).pdf.

20 Samuel Cranny-Evans, Mark Cazalet and Christopher F. Foss, 'The Czar of Battle: Russian Artillery Use in Ukraine Portends Advances', *Jane's International Defence Review*, 24 April 2018, https://janes.ihs.com/Janes/Display/FG_901376-IDR.

21 See US Department of the Navy, 'Navy Maritime Domain Awareness Concept', 2007, https://www.navy.mil/navydata/cno/Navy_Maritime_Domain_Awareness_Concept_FINAL_2007.pdf.

22 John F. Keane and C. Alan Easterling, 'Maritime Patrol Aviation: 90 Years of Continuing Innovation', *John Hopkins APL Technical Digest*, vol. 24, no. 3, 2003, p. 244, https://www.jhuapl.edu/Content/techdigest/pdf/V24-N03/24-03-Keane.pdf.

23 Isaac R. Porche III et al., 'Data Flood: Helping the Navy Address the Rising Tide of Sensor Information', RAND Corporation, 2014, p. xi, https://www.rand.org/pubs/research_reports/RR315.html.

24 UK Ministry of Defence, 'Joint Doctrine Publication 0-30: UK Air and Space Power', Second Edition, December 2017, p. 4, https://assets.publishing.service.gov.uk/government/uploads/system/uploads/attachment_data/file/668710/doctrine_uk_air_space_power_jdp_0_30.pdf.

25 David A. Deptula, 'Transformation and Air Force intelligence, surveillance and reconnaissance', remarks given at the Air Force Defense Strategy Seminar, Washington DC, 27 April 2007, https://www.af.mil/About-Us/Speeches-Archive/Display/Article/143960/transformation-and-air-force-intelligence-surveillance-and-recon-naissance/.

26 US Central Command, 'U.S. Air Forces Central Command Statement on the Shoot Down of a U.S. RQ-4', 20 June 2019, https://www.centcom.mil/MEDIA/STATEMENTS/Statements-View/Article/1882519/us-air-forces-central-command-statement-on-the-shoot-down-of-a-us-rq-4/.

27 Kevin C. Ruffner (ed.), *Corona: America's First Satellite Program* (Washington DC: Center for the Study of Intelligence for Central Intelligence Agency, 1995), pp. 1–2 and 22, https://www.cia.gov/library/center-for-the-study-of-intelligence/csi-publications/books-and-monographs/corona.pdf.

28 See US National Reconnaissance Office, 'The Gambit and Hexagon Programs', https://www.nro.gov/History-and-Studies/Center-for-the-Study-of-National-Reconnaissance/The-GAMBIT-and-HEXAGON-Programs/.

29 Pat Norris, *Spies in the Sky: Surveillance Satellites in War and Peace* (Chichester: Praxis, 2008), pp. 201–2.

30 Piotr Butowski, *Flashpoint Russia: Russia's Air Power: Capabilities and Structure* (Vienna: Harpia Publishing, 2019), p. 16.

31 US Defense Intelligence Agency, 'Challenges to Security in Space', 2019, p. 29, https://www.dia.mil/Portals/27/Documents/News/Military%20Power%20Publications/Space_Threat_V14_020119_sm.pdf.

32 Kiona Smith-Strickland, 'What's the X-37 Doing Up There?', *Air & Space Magazine*, February 2016, https://www.airspacemag.com/space/spaceplane-x-37-180957777/.

33 US Department of Defense, 'Joint Publication 3-12: Cyberspace Operations', 8 June 2018, pp. i–1, https://fas.org/irp/doddir/dod/jp3_12.pdf.

34 Ibid., pp. iv–7.

35 Combined Joint Task Force–Operation Inherent Resolve, 'History', https://www.inherentresolve.mil/Portals/14/Documents/Mission/HISTORY_17OCT2014-JUL2017.pdf.

Chapter One

Chapter Two

Regional Security Drivers

Members of the Gulf Cooperation Council (GCC) face multiple main security concerns, the threat of state-on-state conflict with Iran, the challenge of religiously motivated non-state actors, and the need to ensure internal stability. Not all of the GCC states, however, share the same concerns to the same extent, a fault line that exposes internal tensions between the partner nations. These are strains that now raise questions as to the future of the council.[1]

Saudi Arabia and the United Arab Emirates (UAE) view Iran as a malign influence and a state threat to regional stability.[2,3] Their militaries are now structured to act as a deterrent to Tehran; this until recently was coupled with the assurance of United States leadership in the event of any war. Qatar and Oman view Iran as less bellicose,[4,5] a position that has contributed to the breakdown in relations between Saudi Arabia, the UAE and Qatar, resulting in the last's isolation within the GCC. Oman views Qatar's treatment with concern, given its own approach to the Iranian regime. Bahrain also sees Iran as regionally destabilising,[6] though Kuwait takes a more placatory position.[7] While the GCC might appear to be split equally in its collective view of Tehran, as the two largest military powers by far, the Saudi–Emirati position is dominant.

Reluctant to use military power independent of the US for the last four decades, Saudi Arabia and the UAE are now becoming more extrovert,[8,9] deploying their armies in regional conflicts. This has had political ramifications within the region, and among partner nations further afield.

The splits with regard to how the GCC ought to respond to Iran, the ostracism of Qatar, the strains of the intervention in Yemen, and long-term political disputes within the GCC have become increasingly significant.

The Iranian challenge

Many regional and extra-regional nations are certain that Iran is the hand that shapes many of the destabilising activities that continue to trouble the Middle East.[10] What remains open to interpretation is the

The US decision to designate the Islamic Revolutionary Guard Corps as a terrorist organisation prompted an anti-US demonstration in Tehran on 14 April 2019

ISR & the Gulf: An Assessment

Chapter Two

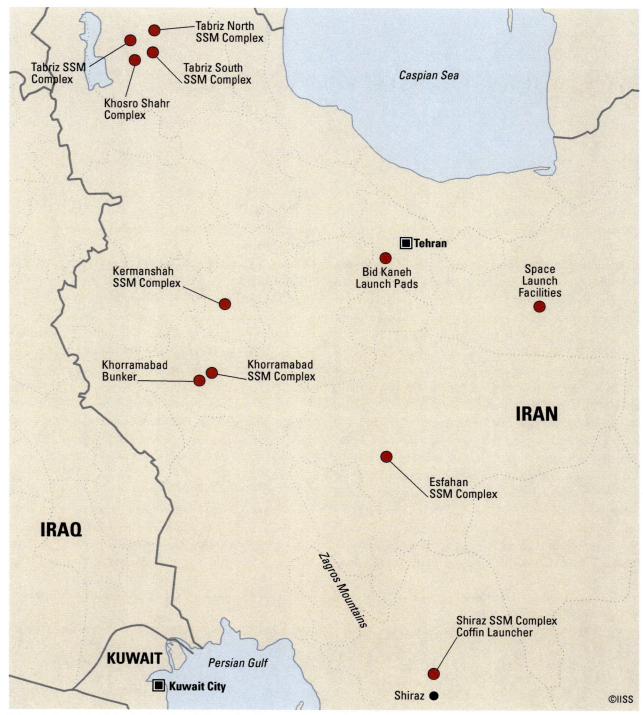

Selected sites related to Iranian ballistic missiles and surface-to-surface missiles (SSMs)

extent to which this is primarily an extension of the revolutionary zeal of 1979 and an intent to export the government's brand of Shia Islam, or mainly a form of forward defence – part of Iran's 'mosaic' approach – intended to keep regional rivals preoccupied with domestic unrest and local conflicts. With regards to external actors, and particularly the US, Iran's aims may be twofold: to encourage enough regional instability for it to preoccupy the focus of the United States' regional partners, but avoid overstepping and risk triggering direct US intervention. The latter could also presage regime change in Tehran.

Building an understanding of the theocracy's military aims and intentions is a regional challenge, and one in which intelligence, surveillance and reconnaissance (ISR) has an important role to play. This is not least of all in supporting analysis of Tehran's actual military capabilities,[11] and the eventual entry into service of new systems, as opposed to that which is asserted by regime rhetoric and accompanying parade mock-ups that may represent only one, or one of hundreds, of a weapon or system. Part of Iran's 'mosaic' defence is likely to try to obfuscate much of the size and capabilities of its inventory, while conveying a domestic propaganda message of military strength built on advanced weapons.

In fact, Iran's military still relies mainly on ageing US-sourced equipment bought during the era of the shah for its conventional forces.[12] As such, in conventional terms, it is comparatively weak when viewed beside some of the other militaries in the region, and in particular Saudi Arabia and the UAE. In redressing conventional weakness, the regime has adopted grey-zone warfare and the use and support of partners to bolster its security. Its strategic backstop is vested in what is the largest regional arsenal of short- and medium-range ballistic missiles, and a now-suspended nuclear-weapons development programme.

Having an accurate picture of Iran's actual conventional capabilities will become even more important in the event that Tehran is able to begin to recapitalise much of its ageing equipment inventory.

ISR can also help provide strategic warning of significant military activity that could be a precursor to an attack. Conversely, it could show that the build-up fitted into a pattern of regularly observed large-scale exercises, and that the activity should at least be considered as part of this wider observed behaviour. In both cases, additional ISR and other indicators could be expected to be used to validate, discount or revise analysis and assessments.

The US position

Increasingly during the 1980s and certainly in the wake of the First Gulf War in 1991, Washington was viewed by the GCC as the guarantor of regional security. US forces have played decisive roles in regional conflicts, and the political protection, military support and the sale of advanced weapons remain a draw for regional states.

The attraction of the US, however, is now less overwhelming. Regional states are taking steps towards more independence in terms of defence and security.[13] While the GCC countries have long dealt with domestic concerns independently, they have been far more hesitant to act alone as regional security actors.

This has begun to change; the Saudi Arabia-led intervention in the Yemeni civil war is the clearest example of this extroversion. Gulf leaders considered the US response to the overthrow of the recognised Yemeni government as inadequate. Washington saw events in the country through the prism of counter-terrorism,[14] rather than as a graver security challenge for the region. For Riyadh and Abu Dhabi, US unwillingness to become more engaged reflected a shift in Washington's priorities, leaving them to act independently. Saudi Arabia and the UAE were at the core of the Arab military coalition that intervened in 2015.

The Saudi Arabia-led intervention in Yemen involves air and ground forces, like this *Hercules* aircraft in Marib province, 12 March 2018

Chapter Two

Ansarullah – an indigenous tribal actor from the north of Yemen, referred to as the Houthis – expanded through central Yemen to the south coast, taking the state's two key cities, the capital Sanaa and Aden, home to the largest Yemeni port. Decision-makers in Riyadh and Abu Dhabi were unable to accept the prospect of the Houthis, a Shia Zaydi group with extensive, complex relations with Iran, taking control of the Yemeni state, which shares borders with Saudi Arabia and Oman.

There is nothing straightforward about the Saudi Arabia-led campaign in Yemen. It is a 'war amongst the people' conflict.[15] The air element of the overall campaign has exposed limitations in the ability to minimise the civilian fatalities and injuries, something that has caused concern particularly in Western states that are weapons suppliers to Saudi Arabia, the UAE, or both. ISR should play a critical role throughout the targeting process, and as such, shortcomings in Yemen point to areas that should be improved.[16]

US 'inaction' in Yemen reinforced the GCC's interpretation of events earlier in the decade. During the Arab Spring in 2011, the US government offered little help to the embattled governments of Hosni Mubarak in Egypt[17] or of the Al Khalifa in Bahrain. Gulf governments were concerned to see that three or more decades of close relations with the US mattered little if rioting broke out in a capital.

Furthermore, the 2015 deal with Iran – the Joint Comprehensive Plan of Action (JCPOA) – to curtail Tehran's nuclear ambitions, was met with scepticism by several GCC states.[18] Combined with the Obama administration's 'pivot to Asia', this signalled that the United States would not be able to focus as much on the region in the future.

Current President Donald Trump shows no greater willingness to involve the US in another war in the Middle East. Rather, and arguably more than any other recent president, he views Gulf relations as transactional.[19]

This is not to suggest that the US will 'leave' the Gulf or the wider Middle East and North Africa region in the coming decades. Yet Washington is faced with competing security demands, of which the Indo-Pacific and the rise of China are the priorities. Added to this, an increasingly assertive Russia has once again meant that Europe and NATO are a renewed focus. Both will absorb political capital and military capability previously available for the Gulf region. This includes some of those high-demand low-density ISR platforms that even the US does not have enough of, such as the RC-135W *Rivet Joint*.

Washington has long encouraged the GCC to take a greater share of responsibility for the region's defence and security. Saudi Arabia and the UAE are now doing so, and learning about the difficulties that this entails.

COUNTRY OUTLOOK

Saudi Arabia

Saudi Arabia views Iran as its rival in a struggle for the political and religious leadership of the region, and the perceived threat from Tehran determines Riyadh's approach to defence and security in addressing state-level concerns.[20] Iran is also assumed by the kingdom to be behind the destabilising activities of most non-state actors in the region, unless otherwise proven.

The ongoing conflicts in Yemen, Iraq and Syria are seen in this light. Saudi Arabia shares long land borders with Iraq in the north and Yemen in the south, both nigh impossible to secure, while it has coastal and maritime security interests on the Red Sea and the Persian Gulf.

Saudi Arabia views itself as the natural leader of the council.[21] Within the GCC the smaller states have tended in the past to try to individually counterbalance Riyadh. The UAE's alignment with Saudi Arabia in isolating Qatar over the last's relationship with Iran and Iranian partners is noteworthy. The Saudi Arabia–Emirati axis was also pivotal to *Operation Decisive Storm*, the 2015 intervention in Yemen.

The US remains Saudi Arabia's most important defence and security partner, though the relationship has become more strained, as the two governments have struggled to accommodate each other's behaviour and stance in the region.[22] The murder of Saudi Arabian journalist Jamal Khashoggi on 2 October 2018 further deepened the rift. Washington, however, accounts for over half of Riyadh's procurement spending, and this relationship remains central to Saudi Arabia's military capability. The assumption in Riyadh is that Washington would come to its aid if there were ever an existential threat to the kingdom.

Even as the US remains its largest single source of military equipment and support, Saudi Arabia is continuing to hedge and further diversify its supplier base. The United Kingdom has long been a defence partner, underpinned by government-to-government defence deals. China and Russia are also sources of supply, with the former in particular emerging in areas such as armed uninhabited aerial vehicle (UAV) systems. Beijing has been the supplier of choice for the kingdom to access technologies that it was unable to access elsewhere – China in the 1980s supplied ballistic missiles.[23] There is also a defence-industrial relationship with Turkey, despite the deterioration in its relationship with Riyadh.[24]

While the UK would almost certainly provide what military support it could to Riyadh were the latter faced

The US remains Saudi Arabia's main defence-industrial partner; here, US President Donald Trump meets with Crown Prince Muhammad bin Salman in March 2018

with a state threat, the relationships with China and Russia appear transactional. This leaves Washington as the ultimate guarantor of Riyadh's security, at the same time as the growing relationships with China and Russia place additional strain on the Saudi Arabia–US relationship.

The Saudi Arabian armed forces are among the best equipped in the region. Unlike Saudi Arabia's regional rival Iran, however, it has until recently had very little operational experience.[25] For most of its existence Saudi Arabia has sought a close relationship with the US to safeguard its security and defence.[26] In the wake of the 1991 war with Iraq, Saudi Arabian defence modernisation for the rest of that decade was driven as much by the desire to reward and lock in the US to the regional security structure, as it was to improve its own capacity for war fighting. The lack of combat experience was apparent in the 2009 campaign against the Houthis, where there was little to no intelligence preparation of the battlespace, a general lack of ISR and an overall lacklustre performance.

The appointment of Muhammad bin Salman, now the crown prince, as defence minister in 2015 ushered in a period of further reform. A joint command is being established, the Saudi Arabian National Guard is being brought within the framework of the military, and there is now an emphasis on professionalisation.

United Arab Emirates

While the UAE views Iran as the regional state threat, its approach is less politically confrontational than that of Riyadh. In part, this is likely informed by its physical geography and the economic risks that a serious deterioration in relations, or the outbreak of open hostilities, with Iran would bring. At the same time, however, the Emiratis' military posture is such that if a war broke out, it could be involved from the off, rather than merely supporting a US operation.

Unlike Riyadh, the UAE does not see Tehran as a rival for regional leadership. Rather, its concern is that a dominant Iran would threaten turning the smaller states in the GCC into satellite regimes. The UAE, like Saudi Arabia, considers Qatar's presumed accommodation and support of Iran and Iranian partners as unacceptable. And as previously indicated, the alliance with Saudi Arabia is significant in that it is counter to the normal pattern of behaviour displayed by the smaller GCC members.

Geography plays a considerable part in the UAE's defence and security concerns. Its proximity to and dependence on the Strait of Hormuz and Iran are significant. A large expatriate workforce and the importance of inward investment for economic development also temper the UAE's stance on Iran, to avoid unnecessarily provoking Tehran.

Chapter Two

The UAE Air Force operates both the French *Mirage* 2000 (left) and the US F-16

The threat from religiously motivated non-state actors is the other main security concern. The UAE believes it is faced with an Islamist challenge to the state; within the GCC, the same can be said for Bahrain and Saudi Arabia.

The UAE's relations with the US are less strained than those between Riyadh and Washington. This is in part because the UAE has participated credibly in a number of US military operations, including in Afghanistan, which has given it the position of a privileged interlocutor. Irrespective of this, any significant drawdown of US regional presence would have a negative effect on the UAE's security over time.

The UAE provides basing for critical US air power such as the U-2 ISR aircraft, RQ-4 *Global Hawk* ISR UAVs, the KC-10 tanker aircraft and E-3 *Sentry*. The US Air Force has also operated the F-22 *Raptor* and F-35 *Lightning* II from the UAE. Across Jebel Ali Port, Al Dhafra Air Base and naval facilities at Fujairah, the UAE hosts around 5,000 US military personnel.

While in Saudi Arabia a hedging strategy is based on relations with the US and the UK, in the UAE, the latter country is replaced by France. The UAE is also courting new regional actors, both in economic and defence terms. Along with Saudi Arabia, the UAE is looking to further develop geo-economic relations with China and Russia, and has acquired armed UAVs from the former when it has been unable to access similar US capabilities.

While the region is known for its expenditure on advanced military systems, this can sometimes appear an end in itself. This is not the case with the UAE. While it has acquired modern systems, this was based on assessed military needs and not on political decisions to procure from a particular partner country. Abu Dhabi Crown Prince Mohammed bin Zayed Al Nahyan, the deputy supreme commander of the UAE Armed Forces, has been instrumental in developing the Emirati military.

Al Nahyan was concerned about two potentially interlinked threats: Iran and violent religious extremism. He sought close relations with the US, reasoning that the US would be an ally in any state-on-state conflict against Iran. But, against intra-state threats such as radical Islamists, or perhaps in states like Yemen today, there was a chance that the US would not want to fully engage. In such an eventuality, Al Nahyan reasoned, he would need an effective military force to defend the regional status quo against threats that would not necessarily muster sufficient concern or support from Washington.

In punching above its military weight, the UAE gained influence within the GCC and further afield. The acquisition of capable military systems was matched, as previously suggested, by the recognition of the value of combat experience in force development. The UAE deployed 1,200 troops as part of the UN Peacekeeping mission in Kosovo at the turn of this century, the only GCC country to do so. Similarly, from 2003 it deployed ground and air units to Afghanistan as part of the International Security Assistance Force.

This growing extroversion has given the UAE the confidence to act not only in Yemen, but also in Libya. These missions are couched in the rhetoric of counter-terrorism. In both operations the UAE is also working with partners, which provide the main presence on the ground while the Emiratis provide special-forces and air support.

Bahrain

A small island state, Bahrain's primary security concern is Iran, at the state-threat level and because of Iran's perceived support for non-state actor activity intended to destabilise the Bahraini regime. Given Bahrain's extensive coastline, as well as its geographical proximity to Iran, maritime security and coastal surveillance should be a priority.

Bahrain supported the isolation of Qatar in 2017, and it also has a long-standing territorial dispute with Doha over sovereignty of islands and waterways. Notionally resolved in 2001, the Hawar and Janan islands and Zubarah town remain a source of friction.

Bahrain hosts a critical US naval base for the Fifth Fleet[27] with around 7,000 US military personnel, but it has also been seeking to deepen relations with other security providers. A permanent UK base was inaugurated in Bahrain in 2018.

The country participated in *Operation Decisive Storm* in Yemen in 2015 and, given the small size of its military, Bahrain's contribution was notable: it committed ground forces and combat aircraft to the campaign, and suffered a number of fatalities.

Given Bahrain's small size, the US remains key to its security, though relations with Washington have become strained over time. This is in part the result of US frustration with what it viewed as the government's failure to adequately address and resolve internal political issues.

Kuwait

Quickly overrun by its larger neighbour Iraq in 1990, Kuwait remains all too aware of its vulnerability to the actions of the larger countries it abuts. Border security with Iraq is a concern; Kuwait has outstanding territorial disputes with both Iraq and Saudi Arabia.

The country's close defence relationship with the US is arguably the least contentious of all of the GCC countries. The Defense Cooperation Agreement that Kuwait signed with the US in September 1991 remains in effect, and is believed to contain relatively far-reaching provisions for US assistance in the event of a crisis.[28] The state continues to host around one-third of all US troops in the Gulf (approximately 13,500 of the 35,000 total) at camps Arifjan and Buehring, Ali al-Salem and Shakyh Ahmad al-Jabir air bases, and Camp Patriot naval base.[29] Kuwait has been a key partner and base for all of the United States' recent regional engagements from the containment of Iraq in the 1990s including *Operation Southern Watch*; *Operation Iraqi Freedom*; the recent air operations in opposition to the Islamic State, also known as ISIS or ISIL; and *Operation Enduring Freedom* in Afghanistan.[30] [31]

Alongside the US, the UK maintains close defence links with Kuwait. It has long provided training, and there have been discussions regarding a permanent UK military base in the state.[32]

While Kuwait did recapitalise its military in the wake of the 1990 Iraqi invasion, and has more recently again invested in modern combat aircraft in the shape of the Boeing F/A-18E/F and Eurofighter *Typhoon*, its force is comparatively small. It did participate in *Operation Decisive Storm* in Yemen, but only for a limited period.

Qatar

Since the mid-1990s, Qatar has attempted to deploy soft power and differentiate itself from its neighbours, in order to balance itself between them. This has led to tangled

US armoured vehicles heading to Iraq following the liberation of Kuwait in 1991

Chapter Two

Five Qatar *Rafale* aircraft arriving at Dukhan Air Base on 5 June 2019

relations with Iran and an array of armed non-state actors across the Middle East. Qatar shares a large gas field with Iran, and as such has an economic interest in regional stability. Maritime security in the Gulf therefore ought to be a priority.

Its approach to Iran, its engagement with Islamist groups and its support for the broad aims of the Arab Spring increasingly put it at odds with its more conservative GCC partners. A change in leadership in 2013 led Bahrain, Saudi Arabia and the UAE to exert pressure on Qatar by withdrawing their ambassadors. A deal of sorts was brokered the following year, but this fell apart in 2017, when the same three countries moved to physically isolate their GCC partner. Trade and travel links were blocked and in the months that followed it was suggested that the US secretary of state at the time had stopped the states engaging in military action against Qatar.[33]

In response, Qatar has sought to use its considerable wealth to buy security. The government has committed itself to large weapons purchases from not only the US but also France and the UK, including those that would boost its air force to a size it will initially struggle to support and maintain without substantial external help. The air force has already begun to take delivery of the French Dassault *Rafale*, while it will also operate the Boeing F-15 and the Eurofighter *Typhoon*. The driving logic behind the purchase of three different types of combat aircraft is clearly political and not military.

Like Kuwait, only with an even smaller population, Qatar reasons that it can only provide limited resistance to a concerted state-on-state attack, and therefore it is best to expand on the one tool that could meaningfully prevent, deter or help with such an eventuality: international alliances. Qatar is also building a relationship with Turkey, buying the *Bayraktar* TB2 armed UAV.

Oman

The Omani approach to Iran is perhaps the least abrasive of all the GCC members, and the state's overall policies are aimed at avoiding taking any position on issues that are considered inflammatory. The uncertainty regarding the successor to the monarch, Sultan Qaboos bin Said, is also an issue.

The effects of the Saudi Arabia-led *Operation Decisive Storm* have, as the campaign has become prolonged, been an increasing concern for Oman along its shared border with Yemen. It did not join in *Operation Decisive Storm* in Yemen in 2015, nor did it contribute to the GCC's Peninsula Shield Force, deployed in Bahrain in 2011.

Among the country's security issues, maritime considerations figure strongly: the location of the Strait of Hormuz and a common coastline with Yemen are among the determining factors. Oman is also host to both US and UK military facilities, and has particularly close ties to the latter. While its military is small, it is well equipped and trained, and has combat experience.

Regional partners

Two further states are worthy of mention in the context of the GCC and with regard to ISR – Jordan and Egypt. The former is a comparatively weak state dependent on oil patronage and goodwill, whereas in the latter the military dominates many aspects of political life. Jordan has well-trained armed forces with recent operational experience. Its special forces have deployed in Afghanistan, and its armed-forces personnel act in an advisory role to some GCC states. It has operated Chinese-sourced UAVs in the armed ISR role. For its part, Egypt has to contend with a complex neighbourhood: Ethiopia and Turkey are strategic rivals; Sudan a troubled neighbour; Israel a cold friend; and Libya a failing state where non-state actors are on the rise. It also conducts counter-insurgency operations in Sinai and in its western desert – operations that have exposed its comparative weakness in terms of ISR, where Israel has provided support. Egypt is also an operator of Chinese armed UAVs.

Iran's military, today and tomorrow

Within the GCC, Bahrain, Saudi Arabia and the UAE consider Tehran to be the single most significant regional security concern. Iran is seen as an exporter of instability through its use of partners, and a threat to the regional order that needs to be countered politically and, if necessary, militarily. Tehran's ballistic- and cruise-missile threat to the Gulf and beyond was addressed in the International Institute for Strategic Studies' 2016 *Missile-Defence Cooperation in the Gulf* dossier. Iran's continuing developments in these areas[34] and its wider military activities, direct and through partners, are a focus of interest for ISR capabilities already in the region. Iran's direction of travel should inform future requirements.

Tehran is faced with a common problem across its conventional forces: all are equipped mainly with ageing and increasingly obsolete weapons.[35] This is all too readily apparent in the air domain, where the GCC states operate a variety of modern combat aircraft such as the F-15 and the *Typhoon*. They are also continuing to recapitalise their air-platform and weapons inventories, either with new aircraft, weapons or both. In contrast, Tehran's most recent significant combat-aircraft purchases were orders for the MiG-29 *Fulcrum* and the Su-24M *Fencer* D from the Soviet Union in 1989.[36] Many of Iran's ageing systems will need to be replaced in the coming decade, otherwise the regime will have to rely even more on its ballistic- and cruise-missile arsenal combined with its use of regional partners to act as guarantors of state security.

Iran's military forces are made up of the Islamic Republic of Iran Army, the navy and air force, and the Islamic Revolutionary Guard Corps (IRGC). The latter also includes the Basij militia and the Quds Force. The last was established in the early 1980s and is viewed as a vehicle for the regime's revolutionary zeal beyond its borders. The establishment of two parallel militaries following the revolution was in part a reflection of the close association of the regular military with the shah's regime, and the suspicion that this aroused. One of the roles of the IRGC was to safeguard the revolution, irrespective of the inefficiencies resulting from running two parallel military organisations. The IRGC is also responsible for Tehran's ballistic-missile arsenal, again reflecting its importance to the regime.

Iran's conventional military posture is fundamentally defensive, even if one of Tehran's aims is to ensure it is a – if not the – regional power. Even so, it has not attempted to initiate a conventional war with any of its regional rivals, nor with the US, but it has sought, and continues to seek, military and political advantage. Up until recently this has been mostly through the use of partner actors, but the

Iran was the only export customer for the F-14 *Tomcat*, which was ordered in 1974 and flown here on Army Day in Tehran on 18 April 2017

Chapter Two

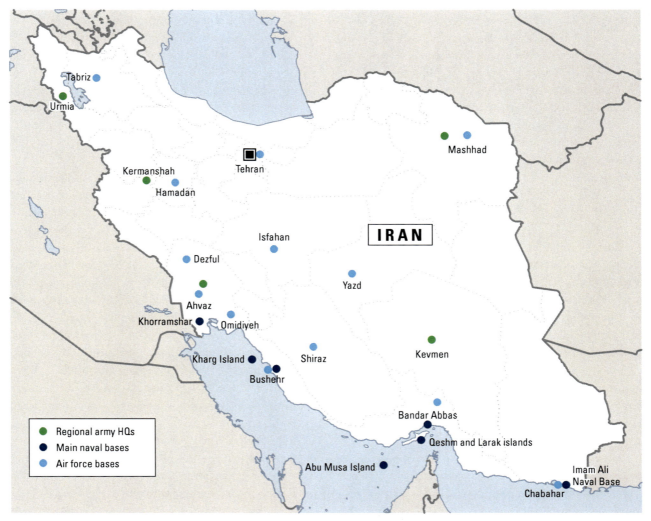

Selected Iranian military bases

regime's increased role in Iraq, Lebanon, Syria and Yemen indicates a greater willingness for direct involvement.[37] This may reflect growing confidence in Tehran that it is able to deploy and use its own military forces, rather than act only through partners, when the circumstances allow.

Sanctions and defence spending

The Iranian economy has had to function under the burden of sanctions for decades, and the imposition of wider sanctions in 2010 and 2018 further hit its economic performance. Counter to the regime's wishes, this also likely curtailed domestic defence-spending ambitions, and the ability to import weaponry. In the first half of this decade annual inflation rose to around 30%[38] and, coupled with sanctions, significantly curtailed economic performance and restricted growth.

Sanctions have been a long-standing element of US policy towards Iran since the 1979 revolution. As concerns over the direction of Tehran's nuclear programme increased, the United Nations and the European Union also strengthened their approaches. The 2006 UN uranium-enrichment sanction, Resolution 1737, was the first in a series that culminated in 2010. In the first half of this decade there was a concerted international effort to encourage Iran to rein in its nuclear ambitions. This resulted in the 2015 JCPOA, agreed by China, France, Germany, Russia, the UK, the US, the EU and Iran.[39] The agreement meant that sanctions would be lifted in stages over a ten-year period, dependent on Tehran curtailing its nuclear activities. Five years after implementation Tehran would be able to import conventional weaponry.[40]

President Trump unilaterally withdrew Washington from the JCPOA on 8 May 2018. The US reimposition of wider sanctions in November 2018 was a blow to the Iranian economy. Government revenue was hit by the ban on oil exports, with inflation rising and the exchange value of the Iranian rial falling as a result.

In the first half of this decade, Iranian defence spending was estimated to be between the equivalent of US$14–15 billion per annum. From 2016 to 2018, spending grew from US$17.4bn to US$22bn, but the figure for 2019 is expected to be around US$17bn.[41] It is probable that defence expenditure will grow in the early 2020s, with figures perhaps of up to US$25bn by the middle of the decade. Factoring in ISR will help provide an answer to the question of how Iran might spend additional funds and which service might benefit the most.

Requirements

The IRGC has become the principal direct means of the Iranian regime exerting military influence beyond its borders. Its Quds Force, long associated with extrovert military action, has been at the forefront of Iran's involvement in Syria.[42] The role of the IRGC's Basij force, by comparison, is mainly internal security. Its ground and naval forces are significant; its air arm less so. Despite this, it is charged with the operation of Iran's ballistic missiles. It is not known to what extent lessons emerging from Syrian operations will influence near- to medium-term procurement requirements.

Iran's missile forces

Iran has built the largest ballistic-missile inventory in the Middle East. Short-range missile systems provide a tactical conventional capability, while longer-range ballistic missiles fulfil the role of a deterrent force. The latter class of weapons was intended to provide the delivery mechanism for Iran's now reportedly suspended nuclear-weapons programme. As such Iran's ballistic missiles are a considerable focus of interest for the GCC, the US and some European countries, particularly those with a regional presence. A measure of Washington's interest in Tehran's missile arsenal is the extent to which the latter's capability features in the US National Air and Space Intelligence Center (NASIC) and the Defense Intelligence Ballistic Missile Analysis Committee's 'Ballistic and Cruise Missile Threat' report. The most recent such report, released in 2017, highlighted Iran's 'extensive missile development program'.[43] The NASIC document also underscores Tehran's efforts to develop solid-propellant medium-range ballistic missiles (MRBMs), along with efforts to considerably improve the accuracy of its missiles.

A shift from liquid-propellant to solid-propellant systems would be significant, posing challenges for surveillance in terms of location. Solid-propellant missiles have advantages in terms of simplicity of use, since the missile does not need fuelling prior to launch. There is also no need for a comparatively complex engine. Presently Iran operates a mix of mobile and silo-based systems. Shifting to an inventory that includes a large percentage of solid-propellant missiles would allow Iran to field a more responsive force not constrained by the need to spend time fuelling the missile prior to firing, whether this be in a silo or using a transport erector launcher (TEL).

Iran's ballistic-missile force is a source of national pride, with a *Ghadr* replica on display in Tehran on 4 November 2017

Chapter Two

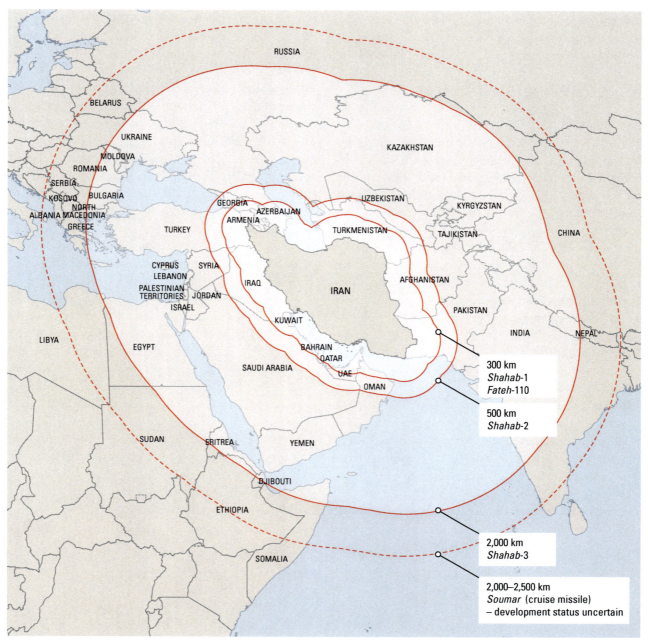

Iran: estimated ballistic- and cruise-missile ranges

The first test of a solid-propellant MRBM was in November 2008,[44] with the missile dubbed *Sajjil*. The *Sajjil*, or the development thereof, is also referred to as *Ashura*. The *Sajjil* has a range in the order of 2,000 kilometres according to the NASIC report. The *Sajjil* likely entered service in 2019, although there is no reliable figure in the public domain as to the number of TELs so far deployed.

Cruise developments

Iran's growing inventory of land-attack cruise missiles further complicates the ISR challenge. ISR assets will not only have to be tasked to identify and locate road-mobile intermediate-range ballistic missiles (IRBMs), but also to track ground-based cruise-missile launch systems. These are even more mobile than ballistic-missile TELs, and could be deployed over terrain that would not be suitable for a ballistic-missile TEL.

Iran's cruise-missile ambitions benefited from the 2000–01 covert acquisition of six Kh-55 (AS-15A *Kent*) cruise missiles from Ukraine.[45] The missiles were supplied without the warhead. The air-launched Kh-55s had been stored in Ukraine in the latter part of the 1980s when it was still part of the Soviet Union. The sale of the Kh-55, which also involved China as a recipient, became public in 2005. Given the previous missile linkage between Tehran and Beijing, it also raised the possibility that there was some cooperation between the two related to land-attack cruise missile design and development.

The first name to be associated with an Iranian cruise-missile project was *Meshkat*, in the 2013 NASIC report.[46] The 2017 report referred to the system as *Meshkat/Soumar*, suggesting that perhaps the system had been renamed, or the *Soumar* was a variant of the original system. In February 2019, Iran unveiled the *Hoveizeh*. This appeared to be the same as *Soumar*, except for a different turbojet engine casing. A cruise missile that appears very similar to the *Meshkat/Soumar/Hoveizeh* has been used by the Houthis in the war in Yemen to attack targets in Saudi Arabia. The shorter range *Ya Ali* cruise missile, first revealed by Iran in 2014, is also claimed to have been used by Ansarullah.[47]

There is much that remains unknown in the public domain as to the extent of Iran's land-attack cruise missile capabilities. There is no reliable information on the nature of the mid-course or terminal guidance of the systems, nor is there information on how the targeting data required for missile guidance is obtained.

Given the attractions of land-attack cruise missiles in that – all things being equal – they offer greater accuracy than ballistic missiles, and their further complication of the air-defence challenge, there is little reason to suspect Iran will not continue to develop and field such systems.

Coastal concerns

Iran's missile relationship with Beijing dates much earlier than the 2000–01 acquisition of the Kh-55s, with the focus on anti-ship weapons. In 1985, Iran ordered the *Silkworm* (CH-SSC-2) from China, followed in the early 1990s with an order for the C-801/YJ-8 (CH-SS-N-4 *Sardine*), and later the C-802. In the early 2000s, Iran also acquired the smaller C-701/TL-10 *Kosar* family and C-704 anti-ship missiles from China. The C-802, known locally as *Noor*, has been further developed by Tehran. The *Ghader* has a range of up to 200 km and the *Ghadir* up to 300 km in the coastal-defence role.[48] In this role, these systems are all mounted in commercial vehicles, again posing a considerable ISR challenge. When the first *Silkworm*s were acquired the US intelligence community raised concerns that, in the event of a conflict, not all of the launchers would be able to be located.[49] This likely remains the case with regard to finding all of Iran's various mobile coastal-defence missile launchers, but effective ISR would reduce considerably the number of launchers and launch sites that would go unobserved. In turn this would reduce, though not eliminate, the overall threat.

Army needs

The Iranian army has more personnel than the main GCC ground forces, but is still dependent on conscription, while its equipment inventory is ageing and in need of replacement. Furthermore, it is likely to be relegated to second place when funding is allocated for ground systems since the IRGC will take priority. The army lacks a capable main battle tank, while its helicopter inventory needs to be replaced.

Iran's *Hoveizeh* cruise missile (on display in Tehran on 2 February 2019) appears near identical to the *Soumar*, which in turn closely resembles Russia's Kh-55 (AS-15A *Kent*)

Chapter Two

Most of the army's heavy armour is based on 1960s and 1970s UK or US designs. The US M60 and the UK *Chieftain* remain in service in various guises, as does the even older M48. Tehran and Moscow have been in on–off discussions over the acquisition and licence manufacture of the T-90 main battle tank for several years, as yet with no outcome. Almost all of the army's helicopters were bought in the 1970s from the US. The AH/UH-1 attack and utility helicopters remain in widespread operation, while some early-model CH-47 *Chinook*s are still in the inventory.

Naval needs

Iran has two navies, the regular navy – the Islamic Republic of Iran Navy (IRIN) – and the IRGC navy (IRGCN). The latter is larger in number and takes the lead in operations in the Persian Gulf including the Strait of Hormuz. It is equipped mainly with small fast-attack craft, many with missile armament. IRGCN naval roles cover the defence of Iran's territorial waters; reinforcing Tehran's claims on disputed territory; and the protection of its Gulf oil infrastructure.

The regular navy's focus is the north Arabian Sea, with the ambition to regularly operate beyond this. Its ailing equipment inventory, however, limits this ambition. In terms of regional threat, its most capable platforms are its three Russian Type 877EKM *Kilo*-class submarines. Its main surface type is the *Alvand*-class corvette, a British design from the 1960s. The *Noor*, *Ghader* and *Ghadir* anti-ship cruise missiles represent its most capable weapons.

Assuming the availability of adequate funding, Tehran is likely to prioritise naval modernisation, although what form such a project would take remains to be seen. It is probable, however, that anti-ship missiles that are even more capable would be an early part of any overall upgrade programme.[50] Iran and the IRIN have used the acquisition of modern anti-ship missiles as a key means of making up for the shortfalls and weaknesses in Iran's naval forces. One critical gap is that it does not currently appear to have an anti-ship missile for deployment aboard its *Kilo*-class submarines, but this is being addressed.

Air-force and air-defence needs

Like the other service arms, the Islamic Republic of Iran Air Force (IRIAF) continues to operate ageing combat equipment. It faces, however, less of a rival in the IRGC than the army or navy, since the IRGC only has a limited air capability. The air force's main role is air defence, with air-to-surface attack a secondary task. It is no longer well equipped to carry out either.

If the air force is to be able to match its regional peers, then it will need to recapitalise key platforms and weapons in the coming decade. Tehran and Moscow have discussed the purchase of the Su-30SM two-seat variant of the *Flanker*.[51] If such an acquisition were to eventually proceed, and the aircraft bought in reasonable numbers, it would mark a notable improvement in the air force. For air defence, it relies mainly on the F-14 *Tomcat*, bought from the US in the 1970s. It has very little ISR capacity in terms of crewed aircraft, but continues to develop UAVs to provide capability.

The air force's only dedicated fast-jet ISR aircraft is the RF-4E, a handful of which may remain in service

Iran's *Alvand*-class corvettes – shown here in the Suez Canal in 2011 – are ageing and based on a 1960s British design

42   The International Institute for Strategic Studies

some five decades after they were first delivered from the US.

The ground-based elements of the country's air defences have also suffered from a lack of investment. Ground-based air defences, however, fall outside the remit of Western sanctions, and Iran was able to buy the S-300PMU2 (SA-20 *Gargoyle*) from Russia in 2015, after President Vladimir Putin overturned a previous decision not to provide the system.[52]

Defence-industry developments

Throughout the era of superpower confrontation, closely watching one another's defence industries was a key role for what was eventually to be called ISR. Satellite imagery of manufacturing facilities contributed to building a picture of the other side's emerging military capabilities, as well as production rates for equipment, including ballistic missiles. In the case of watching Iran this is no different. Alongside its ballistic-missile industry facilities, Tehran is also continuing to develop a broader domestic defence-industrial sector. This is partly the result of an inability to access the international defence market and in some measure a desire to build domestic capacity.

Conclusion

Iran will remain the regional state of concern for the GCC, irrespective of the differing approaches taken to try to manage and contain its behaviour, and the impact of this. Tehran's support of its regional partners and the challenges of violent religious extremism will also be a primary concern of the Gulf countries. Internal tensions, however, mean they are unable to act in unison.

Tehran will continue to invest in its ballistic arsenal, with the emphasis likely on a shift from liquid- to solid-propellant missiles, and on further efforts to improve accuracy. Land-attack cruise missiles will also feature more in its inventory. In addition, if its conventional forces are to not slide towards near irrelevance, then it will need to address, somehow, replacing obsolescent equipment over the next decade.

All of this is of significance to the GCC, and all of this is worthy of attention in relation to the region's ISR capacity.

Notes

1 See Sanam Vakil, 'Iran and the GCC: Hedging, Pragmatism and Opportunism', September 2018, Chatham House, https://www.chathamhouse.org/sites/default/files/publications/research/2018-09-13-iran-gcc-vakil.pdf.

2 *Ibid.*, p. 1.

3 Stratfor, 'The UAE Revisits its Foreign Policy Goals With New Tactics', 13 August 2019, https://worldview.stratfor.com/article/uae-revisits-foreign-policy-goals-new-tactics-iran-houthis-saudi.

4 Vakil, 'Iran and the GCC: Hedging, Pragmatism and Opportunism', p. 13.

5 Giorgio Cafiero, 'Can Oman Pull the US and Iran Back from the Brink of Confrontation?', TRTWorld, 22 May 2019, https://www.trtworld.com/opinion/can-oman-pull-the-us-and-iran-back-from-the-brink-of-confrontation-26865.

6 See International Crisis Group, 'Flashpoint/Global: Bahrain', 19 August 2019, https://www.crisisgroup.org/trigger-list/iran-us-trigger-list/flashpoints/bahrain-0.

7 Gerald Butt, 'Kuwait and Iraq Seek to Defuse Iran Crisis', Petroleum Economist, 20 June 2019, https://www.petroleum-economist.com/articles/politics-economics/middle-east/2019/kuwait-and-iraq-seek-to-defuse-iran-crisis.

8 Simon Henderson, 'Desert Stretch: Saudi Arabia's Ambitious Military Operations', Washington Institute, 16 February 2016, https://www.washingtoninstitute.org/policy-analysis/view/desert-stretch-saudi-arabias-ambitious-military-operations.

9 'The Ambitious United Arab Emirates', *The Economist*, 6 April 2017, https://www.economist.com/middle-east-and-africa/2017/04/06/the-ambitious-united-arab-emirates.

10 Vakil, 'Iran and the GCC: Hedging, Pragmatism and Opportunism', p. 2.

11 Claire Taylor, 'Iran: Conventional Military Capabilities', UK House of Commons Standard Note SN/IA/4264, 24 September 2009, p. 2, https://researchbriefings.files.parliament.uk/documents/SN04264/SN04264.pdf.

12 IISS, *The Military Balance 2019* (Abingdon: Routledge for the IISS, 2019), pp. 340–4.

13 See Abdullah K. Al Shayji, 'The GCC-U.S. Relationship: A GCC Perspective', *Middle East Policy Council*, vol. XXI, no. 3, 2014, https://mepc.org/gcc-us-relationship-gcc-perspective.

14 Jeb Boone, 'How America and the West got it Wrong in Yemen', Public Radio International, https://www.pri.org/stories/how-america-and-west-got-it-wrong-yemen.

15 See Rupert Smith, *The Utility of Force: The Art of War in the Modern World* (London: Allen Lane, 2005).

16 UN Security Council, 'Final Report of the Panel of Experts on Yemen', S/2019/83, 25 January 2019, p. 47, https://www.securitycouncilreport.org/atf/cf/%7B65BFCF9B-6D27-4E9C-8CD3-CF6E4FF96FF9%7D/s_2019_83.pdf.

17 See Sanam Vakil, 'Middle East Perceptions of an America Adrift', The Caravan, Hoover Institution, issue 1921, 28 March 2019, https://www.hoover.org/research/middle-east-perceptions-america-adrift.

18 *Ibid.*

19 See Kristian Coates Ulrichsen, 'Trump's Transactional

Chapter Two

Relationship with Saudi Arabia', Viewpoints, Arab Center Washington DC, 22 March 2018, http://arabcenterdc.org/viewpoint/trumps-transactional-relationship-with-saudi-arabia/.

[20] Ali Shihabi, 'The Iranian Threat: The Saudi Perspective', Middle East Centre Blog, London School of Economics, 7 May 2018, https://blogs.lse.ac.uk/mec/2018/06/15/the-iranian-threat-the-saudi-perspective/.

[21] Jeffrey Martini et al., 'The Outlook for Arab Gulf Cooperation', RAND Corporation, 2016, p. 10, https://www.rand.org/content/dam/rand/pubs/research_reports/RR1400/RR1429/RAND_RR1429.pdf.

[22] See Kamran Bokhari, 'The US-Saudi Alliance', Geopolitical Futures, 21 April 2017, https://geopoliticalfutures.com/us-saudi-alliance/.

[23] 'Saudi Arabia', 1 December 1992, *Jane's Intelligence Review*, https://janes.ihs.com/Janes/Display/jir00446-jir-1992.

[24] 'The Saudi–Turkish Antagonism', IISS *Strategic Comments*, vol. 25, no. 18, June 2019, https://www.iiss.org/publications/strategic-comments/2019/the-sauditurkish-antagonism.

[25] See Neil Partrick, 'Saudi Defense and Security Reform', Carnegie Endowment for International Peace, 31 May 2018, https://carnegieendowment.org/sada/76487.

[26] See Rachel Bronson, 'Understanding the US-Saudi Relationship', in Paul Aarts and Gerd Nonneman (eds.), *Saudi Arabia in the Balance: Political Economy, Society, Foreign Affairs* (New York: New York University Press, 2005).

[27] Congressional Research Service, 'Bahrain: Unrest, Security, and U.S. Policy', 23 May 2019, p. 16, https://fas.org/sgp/crs/mideast/95-1013.pdf.

[28] Congressional Research Service, 'Kuwait: Governance, Security, and U.S. Policy', 4 March 2019, p. 8, https://fas.org/sgp/crs/mideast/RS21513.pdf.

[29] *Ibid.*, p. 9.

[30] *Ibid.*, pp. 7–10.

[31] Benjamin S. Lambeth, *Air Power against Terror*, (Santa Monica, CA: RAND Corporation), 2005, p. 64, https://www.rand.org/content/dam/rand/pubs/monographs/2006/RAND_MG166-1.pdf.

[32] Sian Grzeszczyk, 'Britain "Considering Permanent Military Presence" in Kuwait', Forces Network, 19 February 2018, https://www.forces.net/news/exclusive-britain-considering-permanent-military-presence-kuwait.

[33] Alex Emmons, 'Saudi Arabia Planned to Invade Qatar Last Summer. Rex Tillerson's Efforts to Stop it May Have Cost Him His Job', *Intercept*, 1 August 2018, https://theintercept.com/2018/08/01/rex-tillerson-qatar-saudi-uae/.

[34] See Defense Intelligence Ballistic Missile Analysis Committee, '2017 Ballistic and Cruise Missile Threat', 30 June 2017, p. 18, https://www.nasic.af.mil/Portals/19/images/Fact%20Sheet%20Images/2017%20Ballistic%20and%20Cruise%20Missile%20Threat_Final_small.pdf?ver=2017-07-21-083234-343.

[35] Trita Parsi and Tyler Cullis, 'The Myth of the Iranian Military Giant', *Foreign Policy*, 10 July 2015, https://foreignpolicy.com/2015/07/10/the-myth-of-the-iranian-military-giant/.

[36] Ed Blanche, 'Iranian, Russian Links Ring US Alarm Bells', *Jane's Defence Weekly*, 18 January 2001, https://janes.ihs.com/Janes/Display/jdw00302-jdw-2001.

[37] See Sinan Hatahet, 'Russia and Iran: Economic Influence in Syria', Chatham House, March 2019, https://www.chathamhouse.org/sites/default/files/publications/research/2019-03-08RussiaAndIranEconomicInfluenceInSyria.pdf.

[38] The World Bank, 'Inflation, consumer prices (annual %) Iran', accessed June 2019, https://data.worldbank.org/indicator/FP.CPI.TOTL.ZG?locations=IR.

[39] See Arms Control Association, 'Timeline of Nuclear Diplomacy With Iran', July 2019, https://www.armscontrol.org/factsheet/Timeline-of-Nuclear-Diplomacy-With-Iran.

[40] See Arms Control Association, 'Section 3: Understanding the JCPOA', 2015, https://www.armscontrol.org/reports/Solving-the-Iranian-Nuclear-Puzzle-The-Joint-Comprehensive-Plan-of-Action/2015/08/Section-3-Understanding-the-JCPOA.

[41] IISS Military Balance+ database, accessed July 2019.

[42] See Council on Foreign Relations, 'Iran's Revolutionary Guards', Backgrounder, 6 May 2019, https://www.cfr.org/backgrounder/irans-revolutionary-guards.

[43] Defense Intelligence Ballistic Missile Analysis Committee, '2017 Ballistic and Cruise Missile Threat', p. 23.

[44] IISS, *Missile-Defence Cooperation in the Gulf* (London: International Institute for Strategic Studies, 2016), p. 21.

[45] Roman Kupchinsky, 'Analysis: Kuchma's Ukraine Cruises Back Into The Spotlight', Radio Free Europe/Radio Liberty, 2 February 2005, https://www.rferl.org/a/1057236.html.

[46] National Air and Space Intelligence Center, 'Ballistic and Cruise Missile Threat', 2013, p. 28, https://fas.org/programs/ssp/nukes/nuclearweapons/NASIC2013_050813.pdf.

[47] Jeremy Binnie, 'Saudi-led Coalition Identifies Iranian Cruise Missile Used Against Airport', *Jane's Defence Weekly*, 26 June 2019, https://www.janes.com/article/89521/saudi-led-coalition-identifies-iranian-cruise-missile-used-against-airport.

[48] US Office of Naval Intelligence, 'Iranian Naval Forces, A Tale of Two Navies', February 2017, p. 32, https://www.oni.navy.mil/Portals/12/Intel%20agencies/iran/Iran%20022217SP.pdf.

[49] US Near East and South Asia Center for Strategic Studies, 'Iran's Silkworm Antiship Missile Capability' Memorandum, 2 July 1987, p. 4, https://www.cia.gov/library/readingroom/docs/CIA-RDP90T00114R000700410001-6.pdf.

[50] John Miller, 'Iranian Maritime Improvements: Challenges and Opportunities', in IISS, Gulf Security after 2020, p. 4, https://www.iiss.org/blogs/analysis/2017/12/gulf-security.

[51] Gareth Jennings, 'Iran Eyes Su-30 Procurement and Production Deal with Russia', *Jane's Defence Weekly*, 11 February 2016, https://janes.ihs.com/Janes/Display/jdw61014-jdw-2016.

[52] Nikolai Novichkov and Jeremy Binnie, 'Iranian S-300PMU-2s to be Delivered by September 2016', *Jane's Defence Weekly*, 29 December 2015, https://janes.ihs.com/Janes/Display/jdw60643-jdw-2016.

Chapter Three

Defence-industrial Aspirations and Challenges

The Gulf region has traditionally shopped overseas for its main weaponry.[1] The region has provided a rich export arena for France, the United Kingdom and the United States, with a number of other countries, including Russia and more recently China and South Africa, also garnering valuable business. The reasons are twofold: the region was not capable of meeting its own defence-equipment needs, and military acquisitions form part of broader security relationships.

While the Middle East and North Africa accounted for only 10.7% of the global defence expenditure in 2018, Saudi Arabia alone represented almost half of this total, at 4.9%.[2] In 2018, it had the third-largest national-defence budget in the world, behind the US and China.[3] Saudi Arabia's 2018 defence budget was US$82.9 billion,[4] with almost all of the procurement element of this expenditure being spent overseas.[5]

Internal and external influences are now changing this dynamic. The old, and simple, relationship of purchasing systems off the shelf is no longer acceptable.[6] Defence acquisition is now viewed as having to fulfil needs wider than only buying a system or item of equipment to meet a military requirement: such is the investment now needed in advanced military systems, be it in air, space, maritime or even land platforms.[7]

The Gulf states are building their own defence-industrial bases; why are they doing so, and how are they going about achieving this? Intelligence, surveillance and reconnaissance (ISR) capabilities, including uninhabited air systems, are a feature of industry developments in Saudi Arabia and the United Arab Emirates (UAE). In both countries, investment choices have been influenced by several factors, including US national policy and Washington's approach to the multilateral Missile Technology Control Regime (MTCR). Taken together, these factors have limited Gulf Cooperation Council (GCC) choices and provided an entry point for China to increase its regional presence. Saudi Arabia and the UAE operate Chinese uninhabited aerial vehicles (UAVs) in the armed ISR role, posing policy, integration, and maintenance and support questions. It is a challenge that one extra-regional neighbour in particular has had to contend with: Pakistan's ISR architecture draws upon Chinese and Western-sourced systems, both crewed and

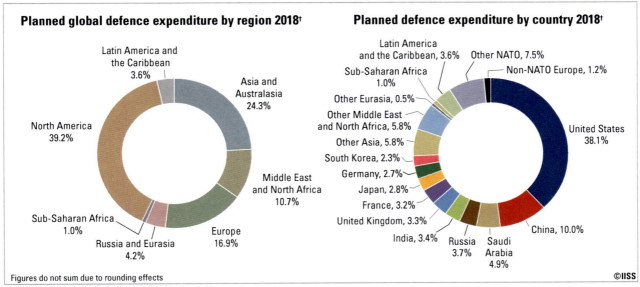

Figures do not sum due to rounding effects

† At current prices and exchange rates

Chapter Three

The Boeing E-3 Sentry deal concluded between the US and Saudi Arabia was part of a wider air-defence upgrade programme

uninhabited, and some of its solutions could prove instructive for the GCC.

Political rationale

There are multiple military and political considerations that may drive a state in developing a national defence-industrial base.[8] One may be what British governments characterise as 'sovereign capability'[9] and French administrations refer to as 'strategic autonomy'.[10] While such phrases are not particularly closely defined,[11] both encompass the sustainment of defence-industrial capability within national boundaries with the broader aim of allowing freedom of action in foreign policy.[12] This can range from specific technologies to the capacity to conduct the design, research and development, and the manufacturing of a complete weapons system. The rationale is that such is the importance of the technology or the platform that the state should not be reliant on an external actor for access to such a technology, or for its support. Such an approach does not preclude multinational cooperation, but seeks to assure access involving, if required, the national ability to develop, manufacture, maintain and upgrade the technologies.

Often, wider political goals also form part of the reason why a state will look to nurture a national defence-industrial base. Naturally, government support is key, since it may be the only customer, at least initially, and the defence-industrial enterprise may be wholly or partly state-owned. The state's procurement policies can also be used to progress national defence-industrial ambitions.[13] The state has the option of directed procurement: rather than compete internationally, a local company will be selected, or established, to meet a specific need.[14] Such an approach involves a greater element of risk: for example, a company established by the state to meet defence needs will have no corporate experience, even if the individuals involved do.

The state inevitably will also shape any national industrial base through its defence and security policy and the types of armed forces, equipment and capabilities it deems necessary to meet such goals.[15] Research and development-funding support can also be used to further direct the sector.

Deals with benefits – dollar pro quo

Such is the scale of large defence acquisitions – combat-aircraft purchases, for example, can now run into billions of dollars – that a buyer can require certain terms and conditions of the seller. This has increasingly become the case as the international military-equipment market has become ever more competitive. More than 130 countries now stipulate what are termed 'offsets'[16] when it comes to purchases in the international market, much of this in the military realm. The World Trade Organization defines an offset as 'any condition or undertaking that encourages local development or improves a party's balance-of-payments accounts, such as the use of domestic content, the licensing of technology, investment, countertrade and similar action or requirement'.[17] There are two general categories of offset: direct and indirect. In the former, a defence manufacturer is required to locate business related to the project in-country based on a percentage of the overall procurement costs; alternatively, the required value could be met by placing business in-country but in non-related areas: defence or commercial.[18] A client state's interest in direct offset is generally indicative of a desire to build a local defence industry, or support one that already exists.

If initially the GCC states were satisfied with the ability to access and acquire what were at the time modern Western military systems, this was because none of the countries had a workforce or the industrial capacity to be involved in either direct or indirect offset.[19]

However, elements of what would become recognised as offsets were identifiable in regional-acquisition programmes as far back as the Saudi Arabian purchase of the BAC *Lightning* in 1966, as the main component of what was called the Saudi Arabian Air Defence Scheme, but it was in the 1980s that offsets grew in prominence. Under the 1985 Peace Shield programme, the US was to develop an air-defence system for the kingdom. This included the integration of ground-based radars, command-and-control centres, and the Boeing E-3A *Sentry* aircraft. Included in the US$3.94bn project was a 35% offset obligation.[20]

It is important to note the sensitivity at the time of the Saudi Arabian purchase of the Boeing E-3 aircraft in 1981. Given the nature of the sale, it was opposed by a pro-Israeli lobby in the US, and the deal required the support of then-president Ronald Reagan.[21] To this day, technology access and release into the region remains a matter of debate in Washington, including key systems relating to ISR.[22]

The 1985 al-Yamamah agreement between the UK and Saudi Arabian governments included a 25% target for offsets.[23] The deal included 48 *Tornado* IDS and 24 *Tornado* ADV combat aircraft, with jet and turboprop trainer aircraft along with a support package. Saudi Arabia established an Economic Offset Programme in 1984,[24] to be followed by the UAE in 1990.[25] UAE offset policy is now covered by the Tawazun Economic Program, which also acts as the regulator for ensuring that foreign companies meet their offset obligations.

Domestic capacity

The intention to develop a national defence-industrial base can reflect not only a state's desire to be more militarily effective but also wider societal aims, including using defence expenditure to support broader industrial goals. This would appear, for example, to be the case with Saudi Arabia's Vision 2030 or the Abu Dhabi Economic Vision 2030.[26]

National capability cannot be assessed exactly, but an adequate sense of a state's capacity can be gained using a basic scale or tier grouping.[27] The lowest tier would be the absence of any national capacity to produce defence material at a meaningful level; the highest would be the ability to design, develop, manufacture and support through-life advanced platforms operated within a digitally enabled environment for all five domains (air, space, land, sea and cyber). The gradations in-between could range from an industrial base capable of only manufacturing build-to-print parts or components, to one that can manufacture and assemble substructures; carry out final assembly; take on licence manufacture and final assembly;

The Boeing F-15 is the mainstay of the Royal Saudi Air Force's tactical combat aircraft fleet, with a number of variants in the inventory

Chapter Three

The General Atomics *Predator* was coveted by some GCC member states, but US legislation stymied attempts to acquire the armed version of the UAV

and finally, achieve a capability of independently meeting all national-defence requirements for advanced military systems. There are only a small number of nations that have developed a defence-industrial base capable of meeting all national requirements, most obviously the US, but also China and Russia. France and the UK also have the industrial potential but have, to a greater or lesser extent, shifted toward a collaborative model with increased interdependence.[28]

Of the Gulf states, the UAE has the most capable defence industry,[29] with the Abu Dhabi Economic Vision 2030 exemplifying the broader aims of developing the local economy and diversifying away from oil. Saudi Arabia is also now looking to move its economy beyond oil dependence.[30] Local defence manufacturing in the kingdom has so far barely registered. In 2017, 2% of defence spending was local;[31] the goal set by Saudi Arabia's Vision 2030 was to increase the amount spent locally on equipment to 50% of the total.[32] This goal is likely to be missed, but the overall aim is to set the process in motion, train and sustain progress. Rather than focusing on a percentage, the aim is to significantly increase local production and begin to develop a domestic defence-industrial manufacturing base. If at the end of the 2020s Saudi Arabia has increased by some margin its capacity for defence manufacturing, this would be marked progress.

The defence-aerospace industrial base and UAVs

Establishing the capacity for defence manufacturing requires a highly skilled pool of specialist labour. This has been a problem for Saudi Arabia and the UAE in that they have comparatively limited workforces with the appropriate skills.[33] As well as the acquisition of advanced military systems from the West, these countries have in the past also brought in the maintenance and support skills required to keep systems operational at acceptable rates throughout their service life.[34] The Saudi government encourages students to pursue science, technology, engineering and mathematics at a higher-education level in an effort to deepen the skills pool, and the further development of partnerships with foreign defence companies is intended to help domestic capabilities grow.[35]

The two suppliers of combat aircraft to the Royal Saudi Air Force (RSAF) are US aerospace giant Boeing and BAE Systems, which has its headquarters in the UK. The RSAF operates the US F-15C, F-15S and F-15SA variants of the F-15 *Eagle* in the combat role, while the *Tornado* attack aircraft and the *Typhoon* multi-role fighter were purchased from the UK.[36] Both Boeing and BAE Systems have a decades-long industrial presence in Saudi Arabia. In March 2018, Boeing and Saudi Arabian Military Industries (SAMI) signed a memorandum of agreement to create a joint venture intended to provide more than half of the

Defence-industrial Aspirations and Challenges

The Missile Technology Control Regime (MTCR)

The 1987 MTCR was agreed initially by the G7: Canada, France, West Germany, Italy, Japan, the UK and the US.[37] The aim was to tackle concerns over the proliferation of nuclear weapons through restricting the main types of delivery systems – ballistic and cruise missiles and UAVs – and the associated technologies required for the design, development, testing and manufacture of such systems.[38] As of 2019, the regime had 35 signatory nations. No Middle Eastern nation is a signatory, nor is China.[39]

When the regime was first agreed in the 1980s, UAVs were in the inventories of only a small number of nations, including Israel, the Soviet Union and the US. They were also in service in far more limited roles and had not been weaponised, although the research and testing of such capabilities began as far back as the early 1970s. The roles, adoption and markets for UAVs have changed markedly in the three decades since the MTCR was established.[40] In part, at least some of the challenges and tensions for US administrations since 1987 stem from the changing nature of the roles and demands for UAVs and the ability, or limits thereof, of the MTCR to address these.[41]

The MTCR established two categories of systems; the first covers delivery systems capable of carrying a 500 kilogram payload to a range of at least 300 kilometres. Category II items are deemed less sensitive, including those systems that have a range in excess of 300 km, but are not capable of carrying a 500 kg or more payload, and related subsystems.[42] In the case of Category I items there is, in the language of the MTCR, a 'strong presumption of denial', while for Category II items there is greater leeway or national discretion.[43] The MTCR, however, is not a legally binding treaty, and as such, signatory nations can ultimately decide whether to adhere to the guidelines on a case-by-case basis. Systems such as the Northrop Grumman RQ-4 *Global Hawk*, the General Atomics MQ-9B *Reaper* and the MQ-9C *Avenger* fall within Category I.[44] The RQ-4 and the MQ-9B have on occasion been approved for export by the US: to Germany in the case of the former, and to the UK for the latter.

required maintenance, repair and overhaul of its military aircraft and helicopters within the kingdom.[45] The creation of the joint venture was linked directly to Vision 2030. Boeing has also been positioning itself to deepen its involvement in Saudi Arabia's development of UAVs.[46]

UAVs are increasingly a core collection platform for ISR, for tactical-, theatre- and strategic-level needs. They have, however, also been a fault line between Washington and its partners in the Gulf, in particular Saudi Arabia and the UAE,[47] and a reflection of internal tensions between government departments in Washington over UAV export policy. Two of the main departments involved are defence and state, with the former the more willing of the two in terms of its view of exports. The US has traditionally

Missile Technology Control Regime membership by year

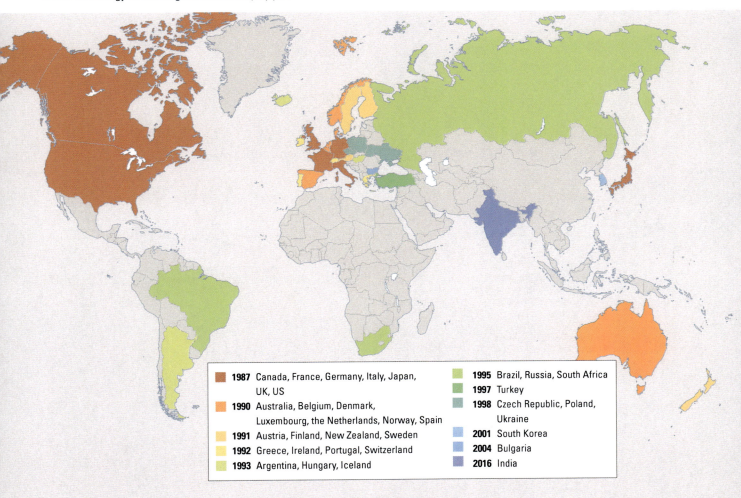

pursued a restrictive approach to the sale of uninhabited systems, particularly those that fall under the auspices of a significant, though non-binding, arms-control regime. This policy was even tighter when it came to the sale of weaponised UAVs.[48]

Diplomatic traffic indicates that Saudi Arabia's King Abdullah raised the issue of buying US UAV systems with president George W. Bush in 2009.[49] The lack of a response was a frustration to the Saudis. Similarly, the UAE had also been pursuing access to US armed UAVs. In 2004, it had rejected an offer by the US to provide an unarmed variant of the *Predator* A, saying that this did not meet its security requirement.[50] The slow pace of US bureaucracy was an irritant, with one request taking two years to elicit a response.[51] Abu Dhabi crown prince, and then chief of staff of the UAE Armed Forces, Mohammed bin Zayed Al Nahyan made it clear to a senior US military official during a 2004 meeting that, were the US unable to provide an armed UAV, then the UAE would look elsewhere to fulfil this requirement. China was among the countries identified as potential partners.[52]

Operating outside the MTCR

China is not a signatory to the MTCR, though there were sustained efforts to include it in the regime in the early 2000s and, in 2004, Beijing had applied to join. By 2009, however, some MTCR signatories did not yet believe that China was in a position to become a member. Membership of the MTCR is by consensus, rather than majority, and therefore even a single opposing vote is enough to block an application. In the case of Beijing, however, there was more than one dissenting voice. One problem was what was viewed as China's less stringent approach to the export of systems and technologies managed by the MTCR, and its associated export-control mechanisms. Beijing's prolonged support of Pakistan's ballistic-missile (and likely also cruise-missile) development in the 1990s and early 2000s was a concern, as was its relationship with Iran.[53] [54]

Discussions regarding Chinese membership continued for most of the first decade of this century, with no result.[55] Beijing's interest in membership has waned, with some Chinese officials viewing the blocking of its efforts to join as politically motivated rather than based on technical concerns. Some Chinese arms-control officials claim that China's export controls are now at least as rigorous as those required by the MTCR.[56]

Beijing not being granted MTCR membership in effect means it is in a far less restrictive position when it comes to the sale of UAVs that fall within MTCR Category I. The failure to bring China into the MTCR, US reticence to sell Category I UAVs to the Gulf region, and the obvious operational utility of such systems combined to provide Beijing with an enviable market opening. This is significant,

Selected producers and armed UAV exports

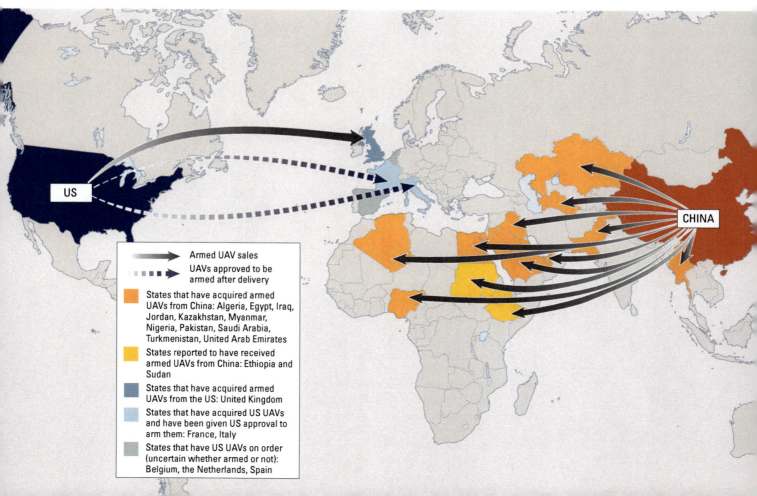

The UAE's UAV approach

In the UAE, ADCOM Systems became a focus for UAV investment as it became increasingly clear in the early 2000s that Washington was unwilling to release MTCR Category I or armed UAVs to the UAE. The largest of the systems developed to date is the *United* 40, a UAV with a range and payload performance that would fall within Category I of the MTCR.[57] The *United* 40 has a payload in excess of 1,000 kg. The design attracted the attention of a number of countries, including Algeria, which in 2013 was identified as a potential customer, while Russia also indicated it would trial the design.[58] However, in the same year, the UAE decided to order the *Predator* XP for the ISR role.[59]

In 2018, imagery emerged confirming that the design was in Algerian military service, known locally as the *Algeria* 54, along with another smaller ADCOM UAV design, the *Yabhon Flash*-20, or the *Algeria* 55.[60] Algeria was already an operator of armed Chinese UAVs, the CH-3 and CH-4 designs.[61] The CH-4 is roughly equivalent to the *Predator*. The CH-3 and CH-4 can be armed with a variety

of short-range air-to-surface missiles and guided bombs, and it is possible that Chinese munitions have also been integrated on the Algerian ADCOM UAVs. The *Namrod* air-to-surface munition was also 'developed' by ADCOM for its UAV family,[62] although ADCOM did not appear to have any previous experience in the design and manufacture of air-launched systems.

When made public in Algeria, the two ADCOM designs were claimed to have been locally manufactured, irrespective of the unusual aerodynamic configuration of the *United* 40,[63] which is sometimes described as a tandem bi-wing design.

Alongside domestic developments and finally accepting an ISR-only UAV platform from the US, the UAE also acquired Chinese armed UAVs. The country appears to have been one of the first export customers for the Chengdu *Wing Loong* armed UAV,[64] and has also purchased the larger and more capable *Wing Loong* II,[65] an armed UAV similar in class and design to the MQ-9 *Reaper*.

---

considering that ISR and armed UAVs have transitioned from a useful support to ground operations to (often) an essential element, without which there can be no green light for an operation, at least in the eyes of some regional ground forces.

At the same time, China's own defence-industrial base was making considerable progress in terms of defence aerospace. While the kinds of systems it could now offer for export in areas such as UAVs were still not the equivalent of the best in the West, they were now acceptable alternatives if access was blocked to US technology.[66] In addition, China was not only willing to sell MTCR Category I-class ISR UAVs, but was also comfortable providing a range of tactical air-to-surface weapons as a part of a package.[67] Unable to access such capabilities from the US, the UAE and Saudi Arabia adopted a dual-track approach, fostering a domestic capability and attempting to access UAV technologies from overseas, with China the main beneficiary. Besides Saudi Arabia and the UAE, Egypt, Jordan and Iraq have acquired armed UAVs from Beijing,[68] albeit with varying degrees of success.[69]

Pushing for change

The US and some like-minded MTCR members have tried in the past to modify the restrictions of the MTCR to better reflect emerging UAV technologies, applications and roles, and to better facilitate their respective industries to address export requirements.

In 2006, the US was seeking support for revised guidelines covering UAVs and cruise missiles that would be adopted in 2007.[70] This would have reclassified some Category I-class UAVs to the less restrictive Category II. The proposal also included revisions to the way in which supersonic cruise missiles were managed, a shift that

would have had an effect on a number of Russian missile systems. Moscow, along with some other states, did not support the US proposal.[71] Modifying how the MTCR handled UAVs such as the *Predator* B had been one of the options identified by US officials with regard to the UAE request to purchase such systems.[72]

A decade later, Washington was again trying to garner support for reassessing how the regime treats UAVs.[73] It submitted a proposal in March 2018 during the MTCR Technical Experts Meeting that would have, if accepted, used a speed threshold as a further means of discriminating between Category I and Category II UAVs. Some larger, longer-range, higher-payload UAVs that would have previously been considered to belong to the first category would, because of their comparatively slow speed – less than a maximum of 650 km per hour – now be covered by the second. Cruise missiles, uninhabited combat air vehicles, and hypersonic systems would remain closely policed as Category I systems.[74]

At the same time, Washington was also unilaterally revisiting its own export-control policy for UAVs. Following a directive from US President Donald Trump that would better align export policy with 'national and economic security interests',[75] revised export guidance was released on 19 April 2018.[76] This would allow for the sale of armed and unarmed UAVs through either direct contract sales or foreign-military sales, rather than only through the latter route.[77] This required approval from the State Department, the Department of Defense and Congress and was a lengthy process, the outcome of which could not be guaranteed. There were several aims of the revised approach including: allowing US companies to better compete in the export arena; avoiding unnecessary tensions with allied nations over technology not

Chapter Three

The UAE has purchased UAVs from China, including the *Wing Loong*

being released; and building bilateral state-to-state relations through the transfer of UAV systems.[78] The change in policy also came with a number of stipulations including that foreign weapons would not be integrated on a US UAV unless approved by the US government; UAVs could only be used for the originally agreed roles unless the US government approved of any change; security protection of any exported system would be to an equivalent level to that of the US Armed Forces; and there would be enhanced end-use monitoring along with unspecified additional security conditions.[79]

Washington's concern was that the MTCR had inadvertently allowed non-signatory nations to gain a competitive advantage by being able to sell systems that would, under the regime, require a 'presumption of denial'.[80]

Uninhabited domain

Developments in Saudi Arabia have to some extent run a similar course. The domestic industry was encouraged to pursue UAV design and manufacture, because of the inability to access US technology. Riyadh also looked to acquire systems off the shelf, with the potential for these to then be built domestically.

The government's King Abdulaziz City for Science and Technology (KACST) plays an important role in Saudi's ISR capabilities.[81] This includes the Saudi Sat 5A and 5B reconnaissance satellites launched in December 2018 by a Chinese *Long March* 2. The two satellites are in low-Earth orbit and are intended to provide high-resolution imagery to the government. The extent to which, and from whom, KACST received foreign support in the design and development of the ISR payload for the two satellites is uncertain.

Given KACST's role in carrying out research and development for the government, including for defence and security, then it is unsurprising that it has also become involved in the design and manufacture of a number of UAV systems. As well as KACST, the government-owned Saudi Technology Development and Investment Company (TAQNIA) is also involved with UAVs. The company has the capacity to manufacture large carbon-fibre aerostructures, including those for UAVs.[82] TAQNIA is also the Saudi partner in a joint venture with Turkish aerospace company Aselsan. The Saudi Defense Electronics Company is focused on radar, electronic-warfare and electro-optical systems.[83] Aselsan produces electro-optical reconnaissance and surveillance systems including the ASELFLIR-200. This is a turreted system suitable for UAVs offering infrared and colour day-only TV cameras, as well as a laser range finder.

KACST showed its *Saker* 1 medium-altitude long-endurance (MALE) UAV for the first time in May 2017.[84] Imagery of the *Saker* 1 appeared to show that it had been fitted with the Chinese FT-9 50 kg guided bomb and AR-1 missile; it also has a claimed endurance of 24 hours. KACST has since shown the smaller *Saker* 2 and *Saker* 3 UAVs, although it is not known whether any of the *Saker* family is in operational service with the Saudi armed forces. KACST is reportedly also involved in a partnering agreement with China covering UAVs.[85] Saudi Arabia has, according to some reports, already acquired 30 CH-4 armed UAVs.[86] The CH-4 was first shown 'publicly' in Saudi Arabia in January 2017 in a display at the King Faisal Air Academy. The following year, imagery appeared online of a CH-4 at King Khalid Air Base in the southwest of the country.[87] This air base is the closest permanent airfield the Royal Saudi Air Force has to Yemen, where Saudi Arabia continues to be involved in its civil war. Several CH-4 UAVs have been lost, with at least some shot down by rebel forces, during operations over Yemen.[88]

Defence-industrial Aspirations and Challenges

Saudi Arabia has ambitions to develop an indigenous UAV industry, with systems such as the *Saker* 1 medium-altitude long-endurance platform

Availability and attrition

Alongside Saudi Arabia, Iraq and Jordan had acquired the CH-4. Jordan is now a former operator of this UAV.[89] It had bought an unspecified number of CH-4s from China in 2016, and also the 'standard' weapons package: the AR-1 and the FT-9. As of June 2019, however, Jordan was looking to sell six CH-4Bs. The proposed sale was part of a wider consolidation of its air-systems inventory, intended to rationalise its overall holdings and to reduce costs. Selling off a system so soon after it entered the inventory, however, would suggest that the customer might not have been happy with performance.

Iraq is also struggling with the availability of its CH-4s. The US inspector general's April–June 2019 *Operation Inherent Resolve* report stated that out of the ten CH-4s the Iraqi military operates, only one was 'fully mission capable'. The cause of the lack of availability was identified in the report as the result of 'maintenance problems'. For Iraq, the lack of ISR UAVs was not limited to problems with its Chinese systems. The same report noted that the more than ten US *ScanEagle* systems operated by Iraq had only generated 'two sorties since March'. The report identified a 'lapse in maintenance contracts' combined with Iraqi personnel being absent from training in the US, and 'signal interference' issues as all contributing to the negligible number of sorties.[90]

Although Iraq's armed CH-4s and ISR-only *ScanEagle*s were near unavailable, there was no reduction in the need for ISR. The latest inspector general's report underscored the demand for ISR capacity, and that the demand exceeds supply. The 'need to monitor Iranian activity in the region, and higher priority needs in other theaters'[91] meant that the Pentagon had to cut the number of ISR assets available to the Combined Joint Task Force–Operation Inherent Resolve (CJTF–OIR). Alongside the CH-4 and *ScanEagle*, the Iraqi Air Force operates the crewed C-208 in the ISR role. It has also begun to use the F-16IQ in a non-traditional ISR role. The CJTF–OIR noted, however, that 'this capability is in its infancy and extremely costly to use'.[92] This would particularly be the case if the ISR tasking were capable of being carried out by a UAV, if one were available.

It is perhaps not surprising that at least some of the countries opting to buy Chinese UAV systems for ISR and ground-attack roles have encountered availability, support, maintenance and loss-rate concerns. The US, for example, has now been operating the RQ/MQ-1 *Predator* and its descendants in combat operations for almost a quarter of a century. The RQ-1 was deployed on operations while it was in effect still a developmental system, such were the advantages of the capability.[93] A downside was that not all of the bugs that would have been identified and addressed in a normal test-and-evaluation programme were fixed before it was pressed into operation. Instead, problems or limitations were addressed as they became apparent. For instance, the actuators used on the MQ-1 had a specified mean time between failure of 150 hours; for the MQ-9 model this was increased to 2,000 hours.

Nor were the improvements limited to the air vehicle. As operational experience accrued, then training could be

Chapter Three

shaped to help avoid many of the human- and ground-related problems that might previously have resulted in the loss of an air vehicle. Other measures such as providing weather updates to the ground-control station about the area where the UAV was being operated also had a positive effect.

China has nowhere near this level of experience, either with regard to its own armed-services operation of UAVs, or in supporting foreign customers in the operation, support and maintenance of its products. China remains a relative newcomer to defence export sales, and in those areas where it has made sales, these have tended to be with older and simpler systems.[94] As previously noted, at least some of the GCC countries look to their defence-equipment suppliers to provide not only the platforms and associated systems, but also to be engaged in the longer-term support and maintenance of these.

Defence-equipment sales are viewed by Beijing as a means of building bilateral relations, much as they are by the US and European countries. Its defence aerospace sector is developing and marketing increasingly capable UAVs across all classes, with an ever-growing arsenal of weaponry also offered for sale as part of any UAV package.[95] Its long-term success, however, will at least in part be determined not only by its ability to sell such systems, but to support its customers adequately during the systems' operational lives.

AN ISR CASE STUDY

Pakistan, technology challenges and China

China's single-largest export customer is Pakistan, and Islamabad has close defence-industrial relations with Beijing.[96] The Pakistan Armed Forces' *Burraq* and *Shahpar* tactical UAVs are very similar to the Chinese CH-3.[97] An initial order for the type may have been placed with China in 2010 following Pakistan's failure to persuade the US administration to provide it with an armed UAV. More recently, a *Wing Loong* MALE UAV was visible in a satellite image of the M.M. Alam air-force base;[98] in October 2018, there were reports that the Pakistan Aeronautical Complex (PAC) and the Chengdu Aircraft Corporation had signed a deal covering the joint production of 48 *Wing Loong* II UAVs for the Pakistan Air Force (PAF).[99] The PAC already works closely with Chengdu on the JF-17 multi-role light fighter aircraft, of which more than 100 have been built so far. The *Burraq* and *Shahpar* share the same airframe, and the difference may be that only the former is fitted with weapons. The missile associated with the *Burraq* UAV is known in Pakistan as the *Barq*, though again this resembles a Chinese weapon developed for UAV applications, the AR-1.[100]

Pakistan has also been faced with the obstacle of integrating or operating in parallel Western and Chinese ISR systems, a challenge that some GCC states may also increasingly face. And like the GCC, Pakistan is using its ISR systems not only in the context of the threat of state-on-state war, but also for counter-insurgency and counter-terrorism tasks. For Pakistan, as with Saudi Arabia and the UAE, UAVS are no longer only an asset, they are also a threat.

UAV operations

When the Pakistan Army began operations in the Federally Administered Tribal Areas (FATA) in 2004 to clear the area of militants, it lacked any kind of near-real-time imagery of what the terrain ahead might hold, resulting in many units being ambushed. In order to begin to address this, the military in 2006 ordered a batch of *Falco* UAVs from Selex (now Leonardo), with ISR the intended primary role.[101]

The air force is the lead service for UAV operations. Rather than adopt the data link offered with *Falco*, the air force adapted the system to use its own, allowing the UAV system to be more easily integrated into its wider digital network. Ground forces now have access to near-real-time imagery from UAVs, providing much improved situational awareness.

The *Falco* is operated by a single UAV flight within the air force, with the unit established in July 2008. A standard mission profile is for the UAV to be flown at around 5.5 km (18,000 ft) allowing the line-of-sight data link to be maintained even in the hilly terrain, with a flight time of between four and five hours. Some of the additional *Falco* air vehicles, purchased in 2013, were assembled using composite structures built by PAC Kamra. The *Falco* acquisition, while initially off the shelf, has been used to support the domestic defence-aerospace sector's understanding of UAV design and manufacture, an approach also adopted by Saudi Arabia and the UAE.

The air force, as in some GCC countries, also operates armed UAVs, and has used them in combat. Operational use of the *Burraq–Barq* combination began no later than 2015. In late April 2019, the current PAF Chief of Air Staff Mujahid Anwar Khan confirmed that the PAF operates both the *Shahpar* and *Burraq* UAVs. The air force describes both UAVs as 'indigenous' despite their resemblance to the CH-3.[102]

Non-traditional ISR

Faced with an urgent need for additional and better ISR as a result of fighting in FATA, in 2009 the air force decided to retrofit a forward-looking infrared onto its Lockheed Martin C-130B *Hercules* transport aircraft.[103] The approach

54

The International Institute for Strategic Studies

Pakistan operates a number of UAVs in the ISR and combat ISR roles, including the *Burraq*

of adapting or using a platform designed for other roles is often described as non-traditional ISR. The UK, for example, faced with a lack of tactical ISR in Iraq, fitted some *Sea King* helicopters with electro-optical turrets, a capability known as Broadsword.

The C-130 work to fit the systems was carried out by the air-engineering depot at the PAF's Nur Khan base. This led to the modernisation of all of the C-130B fleet, and subsequently also a couple of C-130Es, with FLIR Systems BRITE Star and Star SAFIRE III electro-optical/infrared turreted systems. Using the system from around 18,000 ft (5.5 km), the sensor operator can in optimum conditions read a car registration plate. The modified C-130B was used for the first time in the ISR role during *Operation Barq II* (*Lightning* II), which began on 11 October 2009.

Hercules aircraft are also flown along the border with Afghanistan, with the intention of checking for insurgents moving in and out of Pakistan. Islamabad has offered its C-130B/E ISR package to Saudi Arabia. Former PAF chief Sohail Aman, who retired in March 2018, said that the modified C-130s allowed the air force to build up patterns of behaviour with regard to the insurgents, and also assisted efforts to ensure that any engagement met international legal requirements. Aman stressed that any ISR-led operation required a 'proper strategy'.[104]

As aforementioned, the Pakistan Armed Forces had to respond quickly to a greatly increased need for ISR in the counter-terrorism and counter-insurgency roles. The extent of the initial shortfall can be gauged by the comments of another former PAF chief, Rao Qamar Suleman, in December 2007. Suleman recounted that as deputy chief of air staff he had been involved in a situation where there was a lack of up-to-date mapping of the area in which army units had come under attack by militants. Suleman and a senior army officer had to resort to Google Earth on this occasion. Some of the air force's *Mirage* aircraft were ISR tasked, but the turnaround time was over 24 hours for any imagery. It was only with the introduction into service of the DB-110[105] that the air force's ability to use its combat aircraft for timely ISR collection and exploitation markedly improved. The DB-110 from the outset also proved valuable in carrying out what some armed forces term 'intelligence preparation of the battlespace'. When the army renewed its campaign against the Taliban in May 2009 in the Swat Valley, it benefited from Swat and FATA having been mapped using F-16s equipped with the DB-110 in the previous two months.

Operating Chinese and Western ISR

The air force moved to address a significant gap in its situational awareness in 2005 when it picked the Saab *Erieye* to meet an airborne early-warning (AEW) need. Up until 2004, any attempt to acquire a Western AEW platform had been hampered by the US sanctions imposed in the wake of Pakistan's 1998 nuclear tests.[106] Four aircraft were ordered for delivery in 2010–11, with a further three to follow by 2013. The latter part of the deal, however, was delayed, and delivery of the three aircraft only started in 2018. The *Erieye* uses an active electronically scanned array (AESA) radar housed in a canoe fairing above the fuselage. The UAE is purchasing the Saab *GlobalEye*, which uses a further development of the AESA radar fitted to the PAF's *Erieye* aircraft.

At the same time as the Saab system was being acquired, the PAF also looked to its close ally, China, to meet additional AEW and broader surveillance require-

Chapter Three

ments. It came in the shape of the ZDK-03 *Karakoram Eagle* – a Shaanxi Y-8G developed by China Electronics Technology Group Corporation (CETC) with a dome rather than canoe-mounted AESA. The Chinese project may have been begun before the *Erieye* sale was approved by Sweden, and political, financial and dependence issues likely also factored in the decision.[107]

The AEW role was part of Project Vision,[108] initiated by the PAF in 2000 to provide an air-defence environment using an architecture that allowed systems and sensors from different national providers to be integrated. The air force's Project Vision team was closely involved in the specification of the Shaanxi ZDK-03, as well as its design and development. The first aircraft was delivered to the PAF on 26 November 2011 with the No. 4 Squadron formed to operate the type.

Data fusion

A perennial challenge for ISR at the operational, theatre and strategic levels is consolidating data from different platforms and sensors. In the case of Pakistan, not only does it require the creation of a composite picture from Chinese and Swedish AEW aircraft, but also bringing together ground-based radar feeds from US and Chinese systems.

The PAF has four air-defence centres, tasked with monitoring the country's airspace and the surrounding region. Supporting the airborne surveillance platforms are a network of ground-based radars intended to provide all-altitude coverage. High-altitude coverage is provided by the Lockheed Martin AN/TPS-77, Westinghouse TPS 43G and Chinese YLC-2; for medium altitudes, the Chinese YLC-6 is used, and additional radars are used to provide low-altitude coverage. In total, over 20 radars feed information into the composite picture via Generic Mission Control Centres to four air-defence centres. Until the air force began to operate the *Erieye* and ZDK-03, it lacked the capacity to provide adequate overall low-level coverage in some mountainous terrain where radar shadowing had previously been an issue for ground-based sensors.

The Pakistani experience shows that, where necessary, it is possible to build an ISR structure using Western and Chinese elements, but that this also requires innovation and flexibility. As with the Jordanian and Iraqi experiences with the Chinese CH-4 UAV, the Pakistan Air Force has also had to manage maintenance and support issues with regard to the ZDK-03. The air force's development partner for the ZDK-03 was CETC, a large Chinese defence-electronics company with little experience of platform support in the export market. Chinese defence-aerospace conglomerate China National Aero-Technology Import & Export Corporation (CATIC) is now responsible for the support of the aircraft in Pakistan.

Notes

1 Clayton Thomas, 'Arms Sales in the Middle East: Trends and Analytical Perspectives for U.S. Policy', Congressional Research Service, 11 October 2017, p. 3, https://fas.org/sgp/crs/mideast/R44984.pdf.

2 IISS, *The Military Balance 2019* (Abingdon: Routledge for the IISS, 2019), p. 21.

3 *Ibid.*

4 *Ibid.*

5 Kingdom of Saudi Arabia, 'Vision 2030', p. 48, https://vision2030.gov.sa/download/file/fid/417.

6 *Ibid.*

7 *Ibid.*

8 Ron Kane, 'National Governments and Their Defence Industrial Bases: A Comparative Assessment of Selected Countries', Canadian Association of Defence and Securities Industries, October 2009, p. G-13, http://www.defenceandsecurity.ca/UserFiles/File/pubs/CADSI_Comparative_Assessment_National_Governments_and_Defence_Industrial_Bases_2009.pdf.

9 Louisa Brooke-Holland, 'An Introduction to Defence Procurement', House of Commons Briefing Paper, CBP 08486, 28 January 2019, p. 21, researchbriefings.files.parliament.uk/documents/CBP-8486/CBP-8486.pdf.

10 French Ministry of Defence, 'White Paper: Defence and National Security, 2013, Twelve Key Points', 2013, p. 3, https://www.files.ethz.ch/isn/167315/France%20White%20Paper%202012.pdf.

11 Daniel Fiott, 'Strategic Autonomy: Towards "European Sovereignty" in Defence?', European Union Institute for Security Studies, no. 12, 2018, p. 1, https://www.iss.europa.eu/sites/default/files/EUISSFiles/Brief%2012__Strategic%20Autonomy.pdf.

12 Vincenzo Camporini et al., 'European Preference, Strategic Autonomy and the European Defence Fund', Armament Industry European Research Group, November 2017, pp. 15–17, https://www.iris-france.org/wp-content/uploads/2017/11/Ares-22-Report-Nov-2017.pdf.

13 Florence Gaub and Zoe Stanley-Lockman, 'Defence Industries in Arab States: Players and Strategies', European Union Institute for Security Studies, Chaillot Paper, no. 141, March 2017, p. 7, https://www.iss.europa.eu/sites/default/files/EUISSFiles/CP_141_Arab_Defence.pdf.

14 Bilal Y. Saab, 'The Gulf Rising: Defense Industrialization in Saudi Arabia and the UAE', Atlantic Council, May 2014, pp. 33–4, https://www.files.ethz.ch/isn/182154/The_Gulf_Rising.pdf.

15 *Ibid.*, p. 2.

16 International Chamber of Commerce, 'ICC-ECCO Guide to International Offset Contracts', 2019, p. 3, https://cdn.iccwbo.org/content/uploads/sites/3/2019/03/icc-ecco-guide-intl-offset-contracts-web.pdf.

17 *Ibid.*

18 *Ibid.*, pp. 3–4.

19 Saab, 'The Gulf Rising', p. 28.

20 Oxford Business Group, 'Complementary Investments: Defence Offset Programmes Bolster the Economy and Boost Employment and Training Prospects', in The Report: Saudi Arabia 2014, 2014, https://oxfordbusinessgroup.com/analysis/complementary-investments-defence-offset-programmes-bolster-economy-and-boost-employment--2.

21 Charles Mohr, 'Reagan Letter to Congress Chiefs Reaffirms Sale of AWACS to Saudis', *New York Times*, 6 August 1981, p. 4, https://www.nytimes.com/1981/08/06/world/reagan-letter-to-congress-chiefs-reaffirms-sale-of-awacs-to-saudis.html.

22 Lauren Meier, 'House Votes to Block Saudi Weapons Deals Despite Trump Veto Threat', *Washington Times*, 18 July 2019, https://www.washingtontimes.com/news/2019/jul/18/house-votes-block-saudi-weapons-deals-despite-trum/.

23 Jurgen Brauer and J. Paul Dunne (eds.), *Arming the South: The Economics of Military Expenditure, Arms Production and Arms Trade in Developing Countries* (Basingstoke: Palgrave, 2002), p. 206.

24 Mohamed A. Ramady, 'Saudi Arabia: Local Military Content and Relaunching the Offset Program', 26 June 2017, Al Arabiya, https://english.alarabiya.net/en/views/news/middle-east/2017/06/26/Saudi-Arabia-Local-military-content-and-relaunching-the-offset-program.html.

25 Anthony Axon and Susan Hewitt (eds.), *United Arab Emirates 1975/76-2018* (Leiden: Brill, 2019), p. 292.

26 See Government of Abu Dhabi, 'The Abu Dhabi Economic Vision 2030', November 2008, https://www.ecouncil.ae/PublicationsEn/economic-vision-2030-full-versionEn.pdf.

27 Saab, 'The Gulf Rising', p. 21.

28 Bastian Giegerich, Nick Childs and James Hackett, 'Military Capability and International Status', Military Balance Blog, IISS, 4 July 2018, https://www.iiss.org/blogs/military-balance/2018/07/military-capability-and-international-status.

29 Gaub and Stanley-Lockman, 'Defence Industries in Arab States', p. 47.

30 See McKinsey Global Institute, 'Saudi Arabia Beyond Oil: The Investment and Productivity Transformation', December 2015, https://www.mckinsey.com/~/media/McKinsey/Featured%20Insights/Employment%20and%20Growth/Moving%20Saudi%20Arabias%20economy%20beyond%20oil/MGI%20Saudi%20Arabia_Full%20report_December%202015.ashx.

31 Oxford Business Group, 'Localisation Under Way in Advanced Aerospace and Defence Manufacturing in Saudi Arabia', in The Report: Saudi Arabia 2019, 2019, https://oxfordbusinessgroup.com/overview/stronger-together-focus-local-providers-advanced-manufacturing-kingdom-leads-greater-investments-and.

32 Kingdom of Saudi Arabia, 'Vision 2030', p. 48.

33 Gaub and Stanley-Lockman, 'Defence Industries in Arab States', p. 13.

34 Mike Lewis and Katherine Templar, 'UK Personnel Supporting the Saudi Armed Forces — Risk, Knowledge and Accountability', 2018, p. 7, https://www.mikelewisresearch.com/RSAFfinal.pdf.

35 See Thales, 'STEM in Saudi Arabia', https://www.thalesgroup.com/en/stem-saudi-arabia.

36 IISS, *The Military Balance 2019*, p. 366.

37 Missile Technology Control Regime, 'MTCR Partners', https://mtcr.info/partners/.

38 Missile Technology Control Regime, 'Frequently Asked Questions (FAQs)', https://mtcr.info/frequently-asked-questions-faqs/.

39 Missile Technology Control Regime, 'MTCR Partners'.

40 Lynn E. Davis et al., 'Armed and Dangerous? UAVs and U.S. Security', RAND Corporation, 2014, p. 2, https://www.rand.org/pubs/research_reports/RR449.html.

41 *Ibid.*, p. 19.

42 Missile Technology Control Regime, 'Missile Technology Control Regime (MTCR) Annex Handbook – 2017', 2017, p. 2, http://mtcr.info/wordpress/wp-content/uploads/2017/10/MTCR-Handbook-2017-INDEXED-FINAL-Digital.pdf.

43 Missile Technology Control Regime, 'Frequently Asked Questions (FAQs)'.

44 Daniel Cebul, 'Strict Export Regulations May Be Costing US Billions in Foreign Sales', *Defense News*, 18 June 2018, https://www.defensenews.com/newsletters/unmanned-systems/2018/06/18/strict-export-regulations-may-be-costing-us-industry-billions-in-foreign-sales/.

45 Boeing, 'Saudi Arabian Military Industries and Boeing Form Joint Venture Partnership Targeting 55% Localization', Boeing, 30 March 2018, https://www.boeing.com/features/2018/03/saudi-boeing-joint-venture-03-30.page.

46 'Boeing All Over Mohamed bin Salman's Saudi Arabian Defence Procurement Apparatus', Intelligence Online, 7 July 2019, https://www.intelligenceonline.com/corporate-intelligence/2019/07/03/boeing-all-over-mohamed-bin-salman--saudi-arabian-defence-procurement-apparatus,108363928-eve.

47 George Nacouzi et al., 'Assessment of the Proliferation of Certain Remotely Piloted Aircraft Systems', RAND Corporation, 2018, p. 27, https://www.rand.org/content/dam/rand/pubs/research_reports/RR2300/RR2369/RAND_RR2369.pdf.

48 *Ibid.*, p. 13.

49 'Saudi Intelligence Chief Talks Security with Brennan Delegation', 22 March 2009, released by WikiLeaks as Cable 09RIYADH445_a, https://wikileaks.org/plusd/cables/09RIYADH445_a.html.

40 'Shaykh Mohamed bin Zayed Rejects Unarmed Predator Proposal', 27 June 2004, released by WikiLeaks as Cable 04ABUDHABI2113_a, https://wikileaks.org/plusd/cables/04ABUDHABI2113_a.html.

51 *Ibid.*

52 *Ibid.*

Chapter Three

53 T.V. Paul, 'Chinese-Pakistani Nuclear/Missile Ties and the Balance of Power', *Nonproliferation Review*, 2003, p. 1, https://www.nonproliferation.org/wp-content/uploads/npr/102paul.pdf.

54 '(S) Following up with China on Cases of Proliferation Concern', 21 July 2009, released by WikiLeaks as Cable 09STATE76155_a, https://www.wikileaks.org/plusd/cables/09STATE76155_a.html.

55 Haotan Wu, 'China's Non-proliferation Policy and the Implementation of WMD Regimes in the Middle East', *Asian Journal of Middle Eastern and Islamic Studies*, vol. 11, no. 1, 17 July 2018, p. 71, https://www.tandfonline.com/doi/pdf/10.1080/25765949.2017.12023326.

56 Author discussion with a Chinese arms-control government official, March 2019.

57 Richard D. Fisher Jr, 'Dubai Airshow 2013: Adcom Unveils Global Yabhon UCAV', *Jane's Defence Weekly*, 21 November 2013, https://janes.ihs.com/Janes/Display/jdw53911-jdw-2013.

58 Gareth Jennings, 'Dubai Airshow 2015: ADCOM Debuts New MALE UAVs', *Jane's International Defence Review*, 13 November 2015, https://janes.ihs.com/Janes/Display/idr18136-idr-2015.

59 W.J. Hennigan, 'United Arab Emirates Reaches Deal to Buy Unarmed Predator Drones', *Los Angeles Times*, 22 February 2013, https://www.latimes.com/world/la-xpm-2013-feb-22-la-fi-mo-predator-uae-20130222-story.html.

60 Gareth Jennings, 'Algeria Shown to be Operating UAE-developed UAVs', *Jane's Defence Weekly*, 21 December 2018, https://janes.ihs.com/Janes/Display/FG_1406117-JDW.

61 Jeremy Binnie, 'Algeria Unveils Chinese UAVs', *Jane's Defence Weekly*, 30 October 2018, https://janes.ihs.com/Janes/Display/FG_1220142-JDW.

62 David Donald, 'Adcom Unveils Innovative UAV at Dubai Air Show', AINonline, 13 November 2011, https://www.ainonline.com/aviation-news/defense/2011-11-13/adcom-unveils-innovative-uav-dubai-air-show.

63 Gareth Jennings, 'Algeria Shown to be Operating UAE-developed UAVs'.

64 Jeremy Binnie, 'Analysis: UAE's Forward Operating Base in Libya Revealed', *Jane's Defence Weekly*, 27 October 2016, https://janes.ihs.com/Janes/Display/jdw63585-jdw-2016.

65 Christopher Biggers, 'UAE Revealed as Wing Loong II Launch Customer', *Jane's Defence Weekly*, 26 January 2018, https://janes.ihs.com/Janes/Display/FG_726769-JDW.

66 Greg Waldron, 'China Finds its UAV Export Sweet Spot', FlightGlobal, 14 June 2019, https://www.flightglobal.com/news/articles/china-finds-its-uav-export-sweet-spot-457947/.

67 *Ibid.*

68 *Ibid.*

69 Garrett Reim, 'Jordan Military Tries to Sell off "Knock-off" Chinese Drones', FlightGlobal, 4 June 2019, https://www.flightglobal.com/news/articles/jordan-military-tries-to-sell-off-knock-off-chines-458706/.

70 'Missile Technology Control Regime (MTCR): Results of the 5-9 November, 2007 Athens Plenary (C)', 8 January 2008, released by WikiLeaks as Cable 08STATE2034_a, https://wikileaks.org/plusd/cables/08STATE2034_a.html.

71 *Ibid.*

72 'Shaykh Mohamed bin Zayed rejects unarmed Predator Proposal' WikiLeaks Cable 04ABUDHABI2113_a.

73 Congressional Research Service, 'U.S.-Proposed Missile Technology Control Regime Changes', *In Focus*, 22 February 2019, https://fas.org/sgp/crs/nuke/IF11069.pdf.

74 *Ibid.*

75 White House, 'National Security Presidential Memorandum Regarding U.S. Conventional Arms Transfer Policy', 19 April 2018, https://www.whitehouse.gov/presidential-actions/national-security-presidential-memorandum-regarding-u-s-conventional-arms-transfer-policy/.

76 Jeff Abramson, 'New Policies Promote Arms, Drone Exports', *Arms Control Today*, May 2018, https://www.armscontrol.org/act/2018-05/news/new-policies-promote-arms-drone-exports.

77 Kerry B. Contini and Joseph A. Schoorl, 'US Government Aims to Ease Restrictions on Sales of US-Origin Unmanned Aerial Systems', Sanctions & Export Controls Update, 4 May 2018, http://sanctionsnews.bakermckenzie.com/us-government-aims-to-ease-restrictions-on-sales-of-us-origin-unmanned-aerial-systems/.

78 See US Department of State, Office of the Spokesperson, 'U.S. Policy on the Export of Unmanned Aerial Systems', 21 May 2019, https://www.state.gov/u-s-policy-on-the-export-of-unmanned-aerial-systems/.

79 *Ibid.*

80 See Tina S. Kaidanow, 'Briefing on Updated Conventional Arms Transfer Policy and Unmanned Aerial Systems (UAS) Export Policy', US Department of State, 19 April 2018, https://www.state.gov/briefing-on-updated-conventional-arms-transfer-policy-and-unmanned-aerial-systems-uas-export-policy/.

81 King Abdulaziz City for Science and Technology, '"Science & Technology" Produces (38) Drones Characterized by Lightweight, Durability and Being Radar Undetectable', https://www.kacst.edu.sa/eng/about/news/Pages/news535.aspx.

82 TAQNIA, 'Aerostructure Program', https://taqnia.com/en/portfolio/aerostructure-program.

83 TAQNIA, 'Saudi Defense Electronics Company', https://taqnia.com/en/portfolio/sadec.

84 Mohammad al-Sulami, 'King Abdulaziz City for Science and Technology Unveils Strategic Drone Program Saqr 1', *Arab News*, 12 May 2017, http://www.arabnews.com/node/1098376/saudi-arabia.

85 Gabriel Dominguez, 'China to Launch New Strike-capable Reconnaissance UAV in 2018', *Jane's Defence Weekly*, 6 April 2017, https://janes.ihs.com/Janes/Display/jdw65285-jdw-2017.

86 Jon Gambrell and Gerry Shih, 'Chinese Armed Drones Now Flying Across Mideast Battlefields', Associated Press News, 4 October 2018, https://www.apnews.com/1da29d68e3cc47b58631768c1dcfa445.

87 See 'Saudi Air Force CH-4 Drones Revealed', Aviation Analysis Wing, 17 August 2018, http://www.aviationanalysis.net/2018/08/pictures-saudi-air-force-ch-4-drones.html.

88 'Saudi CH-4B Armed UAV Shot Down by Houthi Rebels in Yemen', *Defence Blog*, 30 August 2018, https://defence-blog.com/news/saudi-ch-4b-armed-uav-shot-down-by-houthi-rebels-in-yemen.html.

89 Jeremy Binnie, 'Jordan Puts Chinese UAVs on Sale', *Jane's Defence Weekly*, 4 June 2019, https://janes.ihs.com/Janes/Display/FG_2055286-JDW.

90 See 'Operation Inherent Resolve: Lead Inspector General Report to the United States Congress', 1 April–30 June 2019, p. 46, https://media.defense.gov/2019/Aug/09/2002169448/-1/-1/1/Q3FY2019_LEADIG_OIR_REPORT.PDF.

91 *Ibid.*

92 *Ibid.*

93 See Rojan J. Robatham, 'Predator Acquisition Program Transition from Rapid to Standard Processes', Masters Thesis, Georgetown University, 1999, https://apps.dtic.mil/dtic/tr/fulltext/u2/a566061.pdf.

94 See Daniel Byman and Roger Cliff, 'China's Arms Sales: Motivations and Implications', RAND Corporation, 1999, https://www.rand.org/pubs/monograph_reports/MR1119.html.

95 Greg Waldron, 'China Finds its UAV Export Sweet Spot'.

96 Andrew Scobell et al., 'At the Dawn of Belt and Road: China in the Developing World', RAND Corporation, 2018, p. 138, https://www.rand.org/content/dam/rand/pubs/research_reports/RR2200/RR2273/RAND_RR2273.pdf.

97 Farhan Bokhari and James Hardy, 'Pakistan Inducts First "Indigenous" UAVs', *Jane's Defence Weekly*, 28 November 2013, https://janes.ihs.com/Janes/Display/jdw53971-jdw-2014.

98 Gabriel Dominguez and Sean O'Connor, 'Wing Loong I UQV Spotted at Pakistani Airbase', *Jane's Defence Weekly*, 9 January 2018, https://janes.ihs.com/Janes/Display/FG_713486-JDW.

99 Gabriel Dominguez and Rahul Bedi, 'China, Pakistan to Jointly Produce Wing Loong II UAVs, Says Report', *Jane's Defence Weekly*, 9 October 2018, https://janes.ihs.com/Janes/Display/FG_1145169-JDW.

100 Neil Gibson, 'Analysis: Pakistan's "Indigenous" UAV, Missiles Many Not be as Homegrown as Claimed', *Jane's Defence Weekly*, 26 March 2015, https://janes.ihs.com/Janes/Display/jdw58137-jdw-2015.

101 'Pakistan Opts for European UAVs', *Jane's Defence Weekly*, 7 March 2006, https://janes.ihs.com/Janes/Display/jdw13639-jdw-2006.

102 Gibson, 'Analysis: Pakistan's "Indigenous" UAV'.

103 'Pakistan's Shift to COIN Part 4: Airborne ISR and Airstrikes', discussion thread on Pakistan Defence, 30 May 2016, https://defence.pk/pdf/threads/pakistans-shift-to-coin-part-4-airborne-isr-and-airstrikes.432828/.

104 Author interview with Sohail Aman.

105 Farhan Bokhari, 'PAF to Enhance F-16 Reconnaissance Capabilities', *International Defence Review*, 31 January 2011, https://janes.ihs.com/Janes/Display/idr13683-idr-2011.

106 'US Offers Non-NATO Ally Status to Pakistan', *Jane's Defence Weekly*, 19 March 2004, https://janes.ihs.com/Janes/Display/jdw07375-jdw-2004.

107 Usman Ansari, 'Pakistan Re-equips Squadron with AEW&C Planes', *Defense News*, 28 February 2015, https://www.defensenews.com/2015/02/28/pakistan-re-equips-squadron-with-aew-c-planes/.

108 'PAF's Eagle-eyed View', *Asian Military Review*, 29 November 2018, https://asianmilitaryreview.com/2018/11/pafs-eagle-eyed-view/.

Chapter Three

Chapter Four

The Role of ISR in the Gulf

The security environment of the Gulf and the wider Middle East has significantly influenced how the United States and its allies have developed and employed intelligence, surveillance and reconnaissance (ISR). At all levels, from the strategic to the street, ISR is now an essential enabler in supporting military operations. The presence – or absence – of ISR can be decisive in whether a mission goes ahead. In turn, the Gulf Cooperation Council (GCC) has benefited and drawn lessons from the US ISR systems deployed to and operated in theatre.

Overall, the GCC countries appear to have prioritised the collection element of the ISR process; far less emphasis appears to have been placed on the processing, exploitation and dissemination phases of the cycle. While collectors such as aircraft or uninhabited aerial vehicles (UAVs) are the first and fundamental element of ISR, the process of turning data into actionable intelligence is as important.

The United States and its partner nations' air operations are planned and controlled from the Combined Air Operations Center (CAOC) at Al Udeid Air Base in Qatar. This provides support across the area of responsibility of US Central Command (CENTCOM), which stretches from Egypt's western border to the eastern border of Kazakhstan and covers 20 countries. Five divisions within the CAOC are responsible for overall planning. One division is dedicated to ISR, with the other four covering strategy, combat plans, combat operations and air mobility, respectively.[1]

With the exception of two short and misleadingly one-sided conventional wars against Iraq and Afghanistan, counter-insurgency and counter-terrorism have been the ISR operational focus of the US in these countries for the first two decades of the twenty-first century. Iran and the Strait of Hormuz have also become significant areas of demand for ISR. Together these foci have absorbed, and

The Combined Air Operations Centre at Al Udeid in Qatar provides command and control of air operations in CENTCOM's area of responsibility

ISR & the Gulf: An Assessment

Chapter Four

continue to absorb, a considerable element of the United States' overall ISR inventory, from the tactical, theatre and strategic levels. While the United States' capacity to generate ISR is larger by far than its allies' and partners' in the region, its capability remains a finite resource and demand for ISR is growing.

Despite the anticipation of some in the US ISR community that President Donald Trump's moves to reduce the US military presence in the region would provide some respite from the demands on ISR,[2] recent events in the region and elsewhere have dashed these hopes. The US is now having to contend not only with a resurgent Russia, but also with China, whose rise to global prominence has led to tensions with the US. On 22 August 2019, US Secretary of Defense Mark Esper used his first interview following his confirmation to reiterate that China was the defence department's 'number one priority'.[3] The increased demand on ISR was also implicit in his suggestion that the near-two-decade norm of long low-intensity conflicts was being superseded by the threat of high-intensity conflict against peer or near-peer 'competitors such as Russia and China'. In March 2019, General Curtis M. Scaparrotti, then head of the United States European Command (EUCOM), said he needed more ISR to counter Russia more effectively.[4] These developments only increase the demand on the United States' ISR capabilities, both in terms of hardware and personnel – resources that are already under pressure. Current US ISR deployments in the Gulf region will not be exempt from these demands.

US ISR in the Gulf

The US Air Force (USAF) has had a permanent ISR presence in the Gulf for the past three decades, operating the Lockheed Martin U-2 *Dragon Lady* – a high-altitude ISR aircraft – which has been deployed in the region since 1990. Saudi Arabia hosted what became a larger deployment of U-2s during *Operation Desert Storm* against Iraq in 1991.

Two U-2 aircraft remained in Saudi Arabia until 2001 in support of *Operation Northern Watch* and *Operation Southern Watch* in Iraq. In 2001, the United Arab Emirates (UAE) agreed to host U-2s at Al Dhafra Air Base before the start of *Operation Enduring Freedom* in Afghanistan. The U-2s were joined by three Northrop Grumman RQ-4 *Global Hawk* high-altitude UAVs, marking the type's first operational deployment. The U-2 and RQ-4 types have been based at Al Dhafra ever since.[5]

The USAF's other big-wing ISR platforms stationed at Al Udeid are the RC-135V/W *Rivet Joint* and the E-8C Joint Surveillance Target Attack Radar System (J-STARS) aircraft. Further signals intelligence (SIGINT) support is provided by the US Navy with the EP-3E *Aries* II, with the aircraft operated from Isa Air Base in Bahrain.

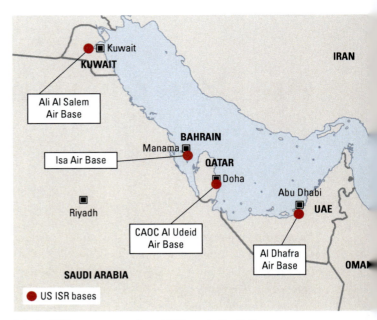

Principal ISR assets are at selected US bases in the Gulf

'Big-wing' ISR

Big-wing ISR has its roots in the Cold War, when it was considered a strategic asset. The term is often used to cover the E-3 *Sentry*, E-8 J-STARS and the RC-135 *Rivet Joint* family of crewed aircraft, with a large number of rear-cabin crew. The tasking of SIGINT aircraft was focused on characterising the radars associated with surface-to-air missile systems to build an electronic order of battle. US emphasis on this capability was reduced following the collapse of the Soviet Union, but intelligence on threat air-defence systems has now regained importance with the deterioration of the global security environment and the increasing risk of peer or near-peer war.

The USAF also deploys the E-3 *Sentry* Airborne Warning and Control System (AWACS) aircraft, with a unit based at Al Dhafra in the UAE. Although the aircraft's primary role is not ISR – it is an airborne battle-management platform – its surveillance capabilities can be employed to inform broader needs. In the Gulf region, for example, the range of the aircraft's primary sensor is such that it could build up a picture of patterns of Iranian air-force activity over the coastal regions and adjacent interior of the country from the relative safety of international airspace.

The U-2 *Dragon Lady*

Begun in 1954 as a CIA–USAF programme, the prototype of U-2 was flown on 4 August 1955, with operational flights beginning in June 1956. There are currently 27 of the U-2S variant of the much-modified original design in the USAF inventory. The U-2 can carry a sensor payload of

The Northrop Grumman RQ-4 *Global Hawk* has been a permanent presence in the Gulf region since it was first deployed in 2001

around 2,270 kilograms to above 70,000 ft (21,000 metres), with an endurance of up to 14 hours, although the longest missions in this region are about 12 hours – the time required to cover Afghanistan.

The U-2 carries an imaging sensor in the nose, either Raytheon's Advanced Synthetic Aperture Radar System 2A (ASARS-2) or Collins Aerospace's Senior Year Electro-optical Reconnaissance System 2C (SYERS-2C). ASARS-2 is primarily a high-resolution mapping sensor, offering eight swath and two spot modes, while SYERS-2C is a long-range optical 'push broom' multispectral sensor that can image in ten wavebands, some of them simultaneously.[6] The U-2 also carries the Northrop Grumman Airborne Signals Intelligence Payload (ASIP), a wideband state-of-the-art SIGINT system.[7] The radar also has two Ground Moving Target Indicator (GMTI) modes, although these are not so frequently employed.

Collection by these sensors is routinely data-linked via a high-capacity Ku-band satellite to a network of Distributed Common Ground Stations in the US for analysis, exploitation and dissemination. The U-2 can also transmit and relay sensor data (including video) to various sites and personnel on the ground, at sea or in the air via two line-of-sight data links.[9]

From above 70,000 ft (21,000 m), the sensor horizon is more than 480 kilometres for SIGINT. This allows the U-2 to collect while remaining well outside defended airspace. However, the aircraft has a defensive wideband electronic-warfare system (EWS), the ALQ-221, which is made by BAE Systems in the US. This detects, classifies and counters threat signals across a wide frequency spectrum using 13 receivers and transmitters. The sensor stand-off ranges provide the aircraft with a level of survivability when operating in a high-threat environment.

The U-2 can also carry a panchromatic Optical Bar Camera (OBC) that provides high-resolution and very wide area coverage, but the wet film is usually airlifted to the US for development and interpretation in a special

SIGINT: COMINT/ELINT

SIGINT includes the collection of communications and electronic intelligence (COMINT/ELINT).[8] COMINT provides the ability to intercept a wide range of communications, from radios to mobile telephones and fixed networks. ELINT covers most other forms of electromagnetic radiation emitted by systems or devices that are not directly related to communications.

Beyond the obvious value of listening in on a conversation, COMINT helps build pattern-of-life activity in high-value targets of interest (especially valuable in the context of counter-terrorism and counter-insurgency operations). Voice recognition can also be used to help identify individuals of interest, often alongside or in support of visual-imagery intelligence.

ISR tactics and techniques can have an action/reaction dynamic, as with all wars. The Islamic State, also known as ISIS or ISIL, increasingly recognised its vulnerability to a range of ISR capabilities, including electro-optical cameras and infrared sensors, and adopted various measures to try and reduce this (including covering walkways in ISIS-controlled towns to hinder the visual identification of personnel).

Chapter Four

US Navy F/A-18Es were used during Operation Inherent Resolve, with ISR support – including extensive U-2 operations – to assist with targeting

centre. This vintage sensor has been flown from Al Dhafra to provide broad-area coverage (a single OBC mission can cover all of Afghanistan). The imagery can provide special forces on the ground with a view of possible ingress and exfiltration routes. The best-known use of OBC has been to monitor the area covered by the Camp David Accords between Egypt and Israel, which the U-2 has been doing since 1978 on flights out of the United Kingdom Royal Air Force (RAF) base at Akrotiri on Cyprus.[10]

Imagery quality is measured on a scale known as the National Image Interpretability Rating Scale (NIIRS), which was first developed by the US intelligence community in the early 1970s.[11] The visible imagery provided by the U-2 is rated between NIIRS 6 and 7, dependent on variables such as atmospheric quality and stand-off range (for a U-2, this can be greater than 128 km). A Level 6 image would allow the discrimination between different variants of military helicopters, or telling the difference between the 9K37 *Buk* (SA-11 *Gadfly*) and the 9K317 (SA-17 *Grizzly*) medium-range missile airframes. Level 7 imagery quality would provide the ability to recognise and categorise 'fitments and fairings' on a multi-role combat aircraft, or to show the launch post on a vehicle-mounted anti-tank missile system.[12]

During *Operation Inherent Resolve* – the US-led mission begun in 2014 to defeat ISIS – U-2s flew daily over Iraq and Syria from Akrotiri and Al Dhafra to assist with targeting. They have also flown, with permission, over some other countries, including Lebanon, where they have monitored Hizbullah. The US is known to have provided ISR support to Saudi Arabia and the UAE at the start of *Operation Restoring Hope* over Yemen,[13] support that could have included U-2 flights.[14]

The U-2 has also flown along the border of other countries, such as Iran. In December 2014, Iranian air-defence forces reportedly warned U-2 flights to turn away from the Tehran flight information region (FIR) boundary, even though this lies at least 9.6 km beyond Iran's sovereign airspace throughout most of the Gulf, and as much as 160 km in some areas.

Although OBC imagery is unclassified, the product of the U-2's other sensors is highly classified. The extent to which it is distributed to other countries – including those in the Gulf – is not known, but it may be assumed that when countries such as Saudi Arabia and the UAE provide basing or overflight rights, the US shares at least some intelligence derived directly from U-2 flights, if not the raw imagery or SIGINT itself.

RC-135V/W *Rivet Joint*

The RC-135V/W *Rivet Joint* is the primary SIGINT aircraft deployed by the USAF in the region, with up to four aircraft being deployed at Al Udeid in Qatar in recent years. The US inventory totals 17 RC-135V/W aircraft, although up to half of these at times have been undergoing some form of maintenance or upgrade.[15] Thus, there may have been times when half of the USAF's available *Rivet Joint* fleet was tasked in the Gulf region. The aircraft has an operational crew of 25, while most of the 17 or so rear crew are normally involved in communications-intelligence roles.

The RC-135U *Combat Sent* – a variant of the RC-135 designed to carry out electronic intelligence gathering on threat system radars – has also been operated in the region, although the USAF only has two aircraft. Beyond the USAF, the Royal Saudi Air Force (RSAF) has two RE-3A/B

64 The International Institute for Strategic Studies

The Iranian missile system sometimes known as *Raad* is medium range, and with more than a passing resemblance to the Russian *Buk* system – it is one of a range of SAM systems of interest to US ISR collectors

(a *Rivet Joint*-based aircraft), while the United Kingdom also operates three RC-135Ws. Ordered by the UK in 2010, the RC-135 was first deployed in the region in July 2014 as part of *Operation Shader*, the UK's participation in the campaign to defeat ISIS. While the RAF fleet is small by any standard, it was a welcome addition to support the USAF inventory: the UK's RC-135s are nested within the broader US fleet based at Al Udeid, and the intelligence gathered is generally shared. The US and the UK have a close intelligence-sharing relationship as part of the Five Eyes agreement that also includes Australia, Canada and New Zealand.[16]

This regional operation of the RC-135W contributes to US intelligence collection on targets such as the Iranian surface-to-air missile (SAM) systems *Raad*, *Sayyad-2*, *Sayyad-3* and *Sayyad-4*. Given the loss of the US Navy's Broad Area Maritime Surveillance Demonstrator (BAMS-D) to an Iranian SAM in June 2019, US and regional interest in Tehran's air-defence capabilities will only have grown further. Iran has and continues to invest in the development of land-based SAM systems[17] – to a greater extent, it would appear, than in naval surface-to-air missiles.

Passive sensors on the RC-135 are designed to locate and help classify electronic emitters such as search and targeting radars. The 'intelligence take' on radars is also recorded for further analysis by electronic-warfare specialists and to support the development of countermeasures. Within the US military, there is a distinction in the tasking of aircraft such as the RC-135 between electronic support (ES) and SIGINT. ES is the result of instruction from the operational commander to meet an 'immediate operational requirement',[18] while SIGINT tasks are generated at the national responsible-authority level. A platform such as the RC-135 is capable of being used to address both kinds of tasking at the same time, if the geography of the emitters of interest allows for collection on the same mission. However, the US delineation between ES and SIGINT is far from always mirrored among other ISR operators. What is common is the potential for tension among those who task ISR, depending on whether they are involved directly in operations or if they have a more strategic overview.

RQ-4 *Global Hawk*

The *Global Hawk* was originally intended to replace the U-2 in the USAF inventory, with the latter to have been withdrawn from service by 2012 (a date pushed back in 2011 to 2015).[19] However, notwithstanding the *Global Hawk*'s impressive performance, there were some areas where it lacked the flexibility and sensors of the U-2.

Compared with the U-2, Northrop Grumman's RQ-4 *Global Hawk* UAV offers a longer endurance (up to 30 hours), but at a cost of less flexible mission planning and inflight re-tasking, and a lower altitude and speed. The *Global Hawk* flies at 55,000–60,000 ft (16,000–18,000 m) compared to the U-2's 70,000 ft (21,000 m). The *Global Hawk* is not equipped with a weather or sense-and-avoid radar and also lacks de-icing equipment, which is not usually a factor in the Gulf, but may be over Afghanistan.[20] Ultimately, the USAF moved to a position of retaining the U-2 alongside the RQ-4 (and given the increasing demands for the ISR that the U-2 provides, the decision to delay its retirement was fortuitous).

Chapter Four

Global Hawk down

On 20 June 2019, the Iranian Islamic Revolutionary Guard Corps shot down a BAMS-D variant of the *Global Hawk* while the UAV was being flown at around 50,000 ft (15,240 m) over the Strait of Hormuz. Like all other *Global Hawk*s, this BAMS-D was not equipped with an electronic-warfare system, such as a passive radar-warning receiver, or an active countermeasures system.

According to CENTCOM, the UAV was 34 km off the Iranian coast when it was hit, but Iran claimed that it was flying inside its sovereign airspace (i.e., less than 19 km from the Iranian

coast), and published what it claimed was radar-tracking data that supposedly proved this. Whatever the truth, the margin for error was small: at this point the strait is only 56 km wide.

A US retaliatory strike was planned and in the process of being executed when President Trump rescinded his order for the attack.[24] The president's reason for his change of mind – that he had not realised that there would be Iranian casualties – was however met with some scepticism; one alternative was that advisers had pointed out the potential for US casualties in any Iranian retaliation.

The *Global Hawk* has two satellite data links, one in ultra-high frequency (UHF) for command and control, and the other in Ku-band for transmission of sensor data. The *Global Hawk* is 'flown' from ground stations in the US (except for launch and recovery). Like the U-2, the UAV sends its sensor data to a network of Distributed Common Ground Stations in the US for analysis, exploitation and dissemination. It can also transmit sensor data via line-of-sight data links (although, again, with less flexibility than the U-2).[21]

The *Global Hawk* has flown many thousands of hours in the CENTCOM region, but at least two have crashed (another four have crashed elsewhere).[22] There have been up to ten *Global Hawk*s based at Al Dhafra, in four different versions. The BAMS-D is a conversion of early-production Block 10 aircraft, with an Automatic Identification System (AIS) receiver and an Electronic Support Measures (ESM) sensor. (AIS is the transponder system used by ships of more than 300 gross tonnage while ESM is an ELINT sensor designed – in this case – to locate and identify ships, especially those that may not be using AIS.) BAMS-D also carries an earlier version of the Enhanced Integrated Sensor Suite (EISS) that equips Block 30 versions. The radar portion is modified for overwater surveillance.[23]

The EQ-4 is a conversion of the Block 20 *Global Hawk* as a Battlefield Airborne Communications Node (BACN). This provides a voice-and-data communications relay for ground forces, allowing multiple users and multiple dissimilar systems to be linked. It has mostly been used over Afghanistan, where mountainous terrain often prevents ground forces from communicating along the line of sight. Until the EQ-4 arrived, this mission had only been performed at a lower flight level by modified Bombardier *Global Express* business jets based in Afghanistan.[25]

The Block 30 is the most numerous version of the *Global Hawk*, designed primarily for overland reconnaissance. It is equipped with a more capable version of the Raytheon EISS, which is a combined synthetic aperture radar (SAR) and electro-optical/infrared sensor (EO/IR) package. A few Block 30s also carry the same ASIP sensor for SIGINT

as on the U-2. A few more carry the Collins Aerospace MS-177A, a multispectral-imaging sensor that has been developed from the U-2's SYERS to offer increased flexibility of coverage. It is being upgraded from seven to ten bands.[26] The Block 40 carries the MP-RTIP radar, which has an Active Electronically Scanned Antenna (AESA) and offers superior-quality SAR and GMTI.[27]

Reaper and *Gray Eagle*: regional workhorses

The General Atomics RQ-1 *Predator* and the MQ-9 *Reaper* are synonymous in the public eye with 'drones', and for good reason: it was the development and operational utility of the *Predator* that moved the UAV beyond a niche capability into a system that found far broader military acceptance. The *Predator* is also the UAV that many in the region aspire to own but none have been able to acquire, with the exception of the UAE.[28]

The *Reaper*'s imagery capability is built around the Multi-Spectral Targeting System B turreted system. This includes television, low-light television and imaging infrared sensors, as well as a laser designator. The imaging sensors provide full-motion video (FMV), which is useful in many circumstances of high value, but time-sliced imagery is often more than adequate and less demanding in terms of bandwidth. There is also the risk that FMV becomes a 'crutch' for military commanders to rely overly upon when it is not required. Weapons integrated with the MQ-9 include the GBU-12 *Paveway* II laser-guided bomb, the GBU-38 Joint Direct Attack Munition (JDAM) and the AGM-114 *Hellfire* missile.

The *Gray Eagle* is a *Reaper* variant; both are used in what is sometimes called the 'combat ISR' role. The USAF uses the MQ-9 primarily in the air-to-surface role and secondarily as an intelligence-collection asset for tactical and theatre-level ISR. The US Army has described the *Gray Eagle* as a multi-mission system. However, as with systems able to perform SIGINT and ES roles, this very utility can lead to tensions over the tasking of a finite resource.

Within the CENTCOM area of responsibility, there are at any one time probably at least three USAF MQ-9

66

The International Institute for Strategic Studies

Reaper squadrons and two US Army MQ-1C *Gray Eagle* companies. The US may have also operated the MQ-9 from a base inside Saudi Arabia close to the border with the eastern section of Yemen at Umm Al Melh.[29] The US is continuing a counter-terrorism operation in Yemen against al-Qaeda in the Arabian Peninsula, and a Saudi base near the border would cut the transit time to the Yemen area of operations for the MQ-9. At least two US MQ-9s have been shot down while being operated over Yemen (one on 6 June 2019, the other on 21 August 2019). Commenting on the 6 June engagement, CENTCOM stated that the altitude of the intercept 'indicated an improvement over previous Houthi capability',[30] which CENTCOM assessed to be due to 'Iranian assistance'. The Houthis, also known as Ansarullah, had previously attempted, unsuccessfully, to engage an MQ-9 using a 9K32 *Strela*-2 (SA-7B *Grail*) shoulder-launched SAM. A Houthi statement claimed that the 21 August engagement had involved the use of the *Fater*-1. The *Fater*-1 missile appears identical to the 2K12 *Kub* (SA-6 *Gainful*). This medium-range missile system was supplied to Yemen in the 1980s by the Soviet Union.

GCC ISR capabilities

There are few big-wing ISR platforms in service with the GCC – the two best-equipped states are Saudi Arabia and the UAE. The majority of the dedicated airborne ISR systems in service with the GCC are either modified light or medium aircraft, or small and medium UAVs.

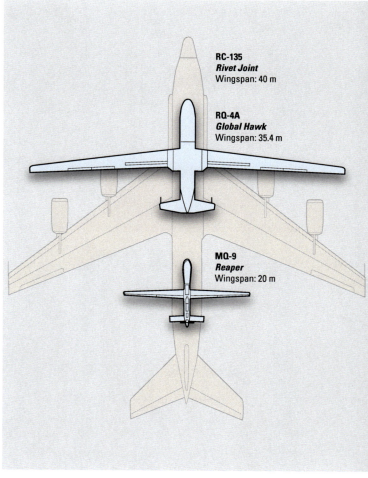

The dimensions of key Western ISR assets deployed in the Gulf

The USAF's *Reaper* and the US Army's *Gray Eagle* variant are in high demand for operations in CENTCOM's area of responsibility

Chapter Four

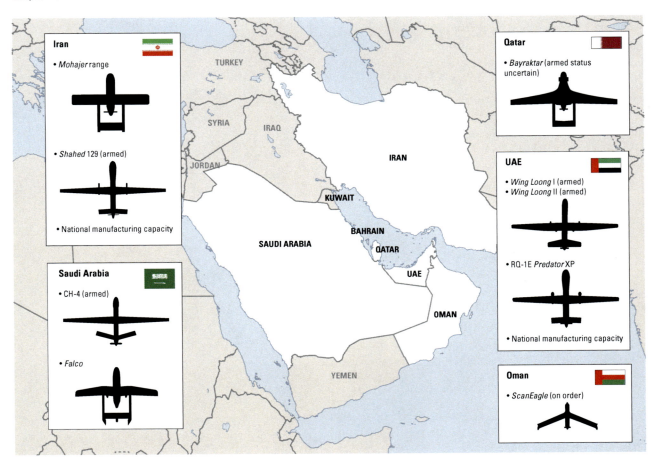

Selected regional UAV capabilities

The most widespread ISR system in service with the GCC air forces is the DB-110 electro-optical reconnaissance payload, which has been sold to 15 countries since it was first produced in 2006. The DB-110 has been purchased by Bahrain, Oman, Qatar, Saudi Arabia and the UAE,[31] and is used by Gulf countries on Boeing F-15 and Lockheed Martin F-16 combat aircraft in their respective inventories. Bahrain, Oman and the UAE operate the pod on their variants of the F-16, while the RSAF has the pod integrated on the F-15 (Saudi Arabia bought ten pods for its large F-15 fleet).[32] Qatar will also operate the pod on the F-15 once it takes delivery of the type. The DB-110 is also in service regionally with Egypt, Iraq, Jordan, Pakistan and Turkey.

DB-110: ISR in a pod

The DB-110 is a podded, dual-band, electro-optical sensor with a focal length of up to 2.7 m (in the visible band). Until November 2018, the manufacturer was known as UTC Aerospace Systems (UTAS). Following UTC's acquisition of Rockwell Collins in November 2018, UTAS is now part of Collins Aerospace. Most customers for the DB-110 have also bought a ground-based mission-planning plus imagery processing, exploitation and dissemination (PED) system from Collins Aerospace.

The DB-110 is based on the Reconnaissance Airborne Pod for Tornado (RAPTOR), which was carried by the RAF *Tornado* ground-attack aircraft and used over Iraq and Syria on *Operation Inherent Resolve* from September 2014 until March 2019, when the *Tornado* was retired.

The DB-110 pod is considerably smaller than the RAPTOR pod, weighs 907 kg and fits on the centerline station of the F-16. The DB-110 offers tactical flexibility, being suitable for direct overflight or stand-off imaging of targets at heights between 250 and 50,000-plus feet (76–15,240 m). Three fields of view are offered: 'super wide', for low-altitude direct overflight missions; 'wide', for direct overflight or stand-off missions at medium altitude; and 'narrow', for medium-high-altitude stand-off missions. The range of the sensor in the visible/near-infrared band is 1,000 ft (304.8 m) at low altitude; about 60 nautical miles at medium altitude; and 5 nm to the horizon (e.g., 200 nm or more) at medium-high altitude. These values are reduced when the second, medium-wave infrared band is employed.[33]

These capabilities make the DB-110 suitable in situations when direct overflight is possible by agreement, or even when it is denied. In the latter case, missions are likely to be planned for fast, low-level penetration to avoid interception, or at medium-fast speed at higher altitudes outside the range of defensive systems such as SAMs.

In each case, the amount of ground-area coverage is superior to most other tactical reconnaissance sensors, including the EO/IR targeting pods that are carried on combat aircraft (such as the Thales *Damocles* pod used by some Gulf countries). The DB-110 also offers considerably more stand-off range than these non-traditional ISR sensors.[34]

DB-110 missions can be planned to offer an area search defined by four corner points or a line search along roads, rivers, rail lines, etc. The DB-110 can also be set for high-resolution 'spot' coverage of previously known targets such as buildings. The sensor also offers target-tracking and stereo modes. Imagery from the DB-110 can be recorded on-board, or it can be relayed via a common data link in real time to ground stations. All the F-15/F-16 customers have bought the Collins Aerospace PED system, which is designed and supplied from the company's UK facility.[35]

During flight, a fighter pilot or weapons-system officer can monitor the sensor's output on their multi-function display, re-ordering or reprogramming targets if circumstances change, such as unforeseen cloud cover or requests from the ground for coverage of new targets.[36] This is sometimes referred to as 'PED Phase 0', where the aircrew carry out imagery analysis in near-real time. (PED Phase 1 is where the exploitation of the imagery recorded is carried out at the operating base, while PED Phase 2 is where imagery is sent to another location for exploitation by the expert community.)

In November 2017, the UAE announced its purchase of the MS-110.[37] This is a multispectral imaging (MSI) development of the DB-110 that offers seven-band collection (visible, blue, green, red, near-infrared, short-wave infrared and mid-wave infrared). MSI allows analysts to see 'colour' and distinguish between subtle features of a target that traditional grey-scale imaging cannot. This helps to detect targets in clutter, camouflage, haze or shadow. Disturbed earth and buried features such as tunnels are also detectable. MSI also provides the limited ability to discern features and objects below the surface of water. The MS-110 pod is the same size as the DB-110, and utilises common ground-support and exploitation systems.[38] (Existing DB-110s can be upgraded to MS-110.)

In partnership with the UK facility of Leonardo's Electronics Division, Collins Aerospace has designed an imaging radar pod known as TacSAR (Tactical Synthetic Aperture) that has the same dimensions and mostly compatible avionics. A multi-mode AESA replaces the optics and allows near-photographic-quality imagery to be collected in all weather conditions. Collins Aerospace reports considerable interest in the TacSAR system, and expects to secure a launch customer within the next 12 months.[39]

Starting in 2006, Collins Aerospace has conducted three trials of the DB-110 sensor on the MQ-9 *Reaper*. The second trial in 2013 used a new lightweight pod, which was enhanced for the most recent trial in 2017 on a US Air National Guard (ANG) MQ-9, a trial that was described as an operational assessment. The ANG plans to equip a number of MQ-9 squadrons with the DB-110. They would primarily use the MQ-9/MS-110 combination to conduct wide-area assessments of natural disasters such as hurricanes, wildfires and floods.[40]

The DB-110 or MS-110 sensor could be fitted to other UAVs and Collins Aerospace said that as of the third quarter of 2019 it was in discussion with several customers. Whether they include countries in the Gulf is not known, but Collins Aerospace is hoping to interest the UK in adding the sensor to its forthcoming fleet of *Protector* UAVs (a development of the MQ-9 with longer range and that can be certified for operation in non-segregated airspace).[41]

As for other platforms, the UAE has bought two Bombardier *Global* 6000 business jets, possibly with the DB-110 installed, alongside a SIGINT system. India has fitted the DB-110 to a *Global* 5000 business jet. Collins Aerospace has also suggested that the sensor could be added to larger aircraft such as airlifters, tankers and maritime-patrol aircraft (MPA). Japan has already added the DB-110 to P-3 *Orion* MPAs.[42]

Saudi Arabia

The RSAF has two RE-3 Tactical Airborne Surveillance System aircraft in its inventory. The RE-3s are used for SIGINT, and following an upgrade, one aircraft now externally resembles the RC-135W in terms of configuration. The Saudi aircraft are likely capable of both COMINT and ELINT. The two aircraft are flown by the 19th Squadron and notionally based at Prince Sultan Air Base in central Saudi Arabia.

The RSAF operates *King Air* 350s in the ISR role as part of the same unit with the RE-3s. The first *King Air*s in the ISR role may have been delivered to the RSAF in 2011,[43] with the aircraft fitted with a range of sensors. There have been subsequent Saudi Arabian orders for ISR-modified *King Air*s, but the number in the Saudi inventory and the operator (or operators) is not known. The 2011 acquisition of the *King Air* 350s for the ISR role may have been spurred in part by Saudi Arabia's inability to purchase the US *Predator* or *Reaper*. This situation also drove the kingdom's interest in developing its own UAVs, as well as sourcing these from China.

Chapter Four

Space: the next ISR frontier for the GCC

The value and national prestige of space-based ISR has long been recognised by Saudi Arabia and the UAE. For the past two decades both countries have had access to commercial providers of high-resolution satellite imagery, and are now complementing this with national resources.

The UAE has set the pace for developing a national military space capability with its *Falcon Eye* satellites, which were developed for the UAE by Airbus Defence and Space under a 2014 contract that also involves Thales Alenia Space.[45] Based on the *Pleiades*-HR satellite design, the *Falcon Eye* optical payload can provide imagery resolution of 0.7 m across a 20 km swath. *Falcon Eye* imagery will be processed at the air force's Space Reconnaissance Center, located at Al Dhafra Air Base in Abu Dhabi. The base, which was established in the early 1990s,[46] is a centre for ISR processing and exploitation, including imagery from the air force's reconnaissance-pod equipped fighter aircraft.

There has been the occasional setback, such as the loss of the *Falcon Eye* 1 reconnaissance satellite on 10 July 2019,[47] when the *Vega* rocket carrying the UAE satellite failed, with a possible malfunction of the second stage suggested as the potential cause.[48] As of the third quarter of 2019, the launch of *Falcon Eye* 2 was still planned to take place before the end of the year.

The UAE was also the first of the GCC countries to establish a national space agency (in 2014).[49] In December 2018, the Saudi government announced that it would set up the Saudi Space Agency as a focus for all space-related activities.[50] It will work alongside the King Abdulaziz City for Science and Technology, which has previously been the lead for space activities in the kingdom. This work has included the SaudiSat5A/B Earth-observation satellites launched in December 2018. A Chinese *Long March* 2D (CZ-2D) was the launcher for the SaudiSats.

Reflecting its overall space ambition, the UAE has also led the formation of the Arab Space Coordination Group.[51] Established in March 2019, this group includes all of the GCC countries bar Qatar, along with Algeria, Egypt, Jordan, Lebanon, Morocco and Sudan. The group will focus on civil space applications and its first project is Satellite 813, an Earth-observation platform to be developed by the UAE that will be used to look at the environment and the effects of climate change.

Saudi Arabia operates an unconfirmed number of the China Aerospace Science and Technology Corporation CH-4A/4B UAV. The CH-4 is in the same class as the *Reaper* (a resemblance that is often remarked upon). The CH-4A is configured primarily for the ISR role, carrying EO/IR sensors in a chin-mounted turret. The CH-4B is configured for the air-to-surface role, exchanging endurance for increased payload. In the ISR role, the CH-4A has an endurance of up to 30 hours, although the CH-4B is only capable of 13 hours. A 2018 report suggested that at least 30 CH-4s had been exported to Saudi Arabia.[44]

The Saudi CH-4Bs have been displayed with the 45 kg short-range AR-1 semi-active laser-guided missile and the 50 kg FT-9 precision-guided bomb. Accuracy of the former is claimed to be 1.5 m,[52] while the latter's accuracy is given as 3 m using semi-active laser guidance.[53]

UAE

The UAE is in the process of recapitalising its crewed ISR platforms, with the acquisition of a multi-mission sensor aircraft from Sweden, the *GlobalEye*,[54] and a SIGINT plat-

The Chinese *Wing Loong* family has already been exported to the UAE, with the UAV offered with a large number of air-to-surface weapons capable of being integrated

form through what is known as Project Dolphin.[55] These included the acquisition of a multi-mission-capable airborne early-warning and control (AEW&C) aircraft, and a multi-role ISR aircraft fitted with SIGINT and electro-optical payloads.

As with Saudi Arabia, the UAE also operates Chinese UAVs, but these are part of the *Wing Loong* family. The UAE Air Force acquired an undisclosed number of the Chengdu *Wing Loong* I around 2014,[56] and is also believed to be a customer for the larger and more capable *Wing Loong* II. As with the RSAF's CH-4, the *Wing Loong* is fitted with an EO/IR turret and can carry a range of air-to-surface munitions, including the *Blue Arrow*-7 (a semi-active laser-guided air-to-surface missile known in Chinese service as the AKD-10). The missile weighs 47 kg and has a range of up to 7 km. The *Wing Loong* I and II have an endurance of 20 hours.

Qatar has also purchased UAVs, in its case from Turkey, with the *Bayraktar* TB2. Delivery of the systems likely took place in the first or second quarter of 2019.[57]

GlobalEye

Even though the UAE was already a Swedish AEW customer, the choice of the Saab *GlobalEye* on 9 November 2015 as the winner of the air force's long-running AEW&C requirement was perhaps a surprise, not least of all because the UAE was the launch customer for the aircraft.[58] There had been little publicity regarding the *GlobalEye* Swing Role Surveillance System before Saab garnered the US$1.27 billion contract for two aircraft from the Emiratis.[59] The contract value covered the purchase and conversion of two Bombardier 6000 business jets, a ground-surveillance system, security, preparations for basing the aircraft in country, and training and spares. The original contract was followed in February 2016 with the order for a third aircraft at the additional cost of US$236 million.[60]

Two US platforms were in competition with the relatively unknown Saab offering. Northrop Grumman proposed a version of the E-2 *Hawkeye*, while Boeing had bid a variant of the E-7. Choosing a system from Sweden, rather than the US (which remains the Emirates' most important defence partner in security terms) may have been unexpected, but it also underscored the UAE's interest in maintaining a diversity of suppliers and avoiding reliance on Washington. (Saudi Arabia also operates Saab-developed AEW aircraft.)[61]

Saab's history with the UAE also goes some way to explaining why the UAE chose the Swedish company. Saab's relationship with the UAE in the AEW&C role began in 2009 when the UAE Air Force ordered two second-hand AEW Saab 340s,[62] which were fitted with the FSR 890 mission suite. This was an interim solution to provide low-level coverage that ground-based radars could not meet at adequate detection ranges. At the time, the UAE Air Force had a long-standing requirement for an AEW and multi-mission aircraft, and wanted a customised system to fit in with its concept of operations, rather than buy off-the-shelf from the US, which may have come with technology restrictions that can sometimes hamper US export efforts.

Work on a prototype platform commenced with the signature of the *GlobalEye* contract in November 2015, by which time Saab had a better understanding of the UAE's concept of operations for the aircraft. The then UAE Air Force and Air Defence commander Major-General Staff Pilot Ibrahim Naser al Alawi said that the 2009 Saab 340 acquisition 'was part of a plan to evaluate [the *Erieye*] for its future requirements on a permanent solution ... We were looking for a state of the art system and *GlobalEye* confirmed that capability with an outstanding performance.' The *GlobalEye* can extend low-level coverage up to ten times further than ground-based radar.[63] This equates to the defending force having up to an extra 20 minutes to prepare.

At the heart of the *GlobalEye*'s air-to-air capability is the *Erieye* extended range AESA multi-mode radar. This is housed in a canoe on the top of the aircraft. Saab claims that the target-detection ranges for the radar are more than 215 nm (400 km).[64] The mission system includes five workstations in the cabin that are reconfigurable, with each capable of being used to cover any of the three domains (air, land or sea), although an operator would typically have a dedicated role. For an air-defence mission, for example, three workstations would likely be configured for fighter controllers, one for an electronic-support measures officer and one for the mission commander.

Given the UAE's considerable coastline, and the nature of the waterway that it borders, the maritime-surveillance capability of the aircraft is also important. The *GlobalEye*'s maritime-surveillance capability is provided by several sensors: the Leonardo *Seaspray* 7500, the electro-optical turret, and also the AIS. In a benign environment, the aircraft can be operated at 5,000 ft (1,524 m), allowing for the identification and examination of even very small surface maritime vessels of interest. In a higher-threat environment, rather than risk such a high-value asset, information on the target of interest would be handed off for tasking with a more expendable, or less vulnerable, platform (such as a UAV).

For the identification of air-to-air tracks, the *GlobalEye* is equipped with both a military identification friend-or-foe system and the commercial Automatic Dependent System–Broadcast (ADS–B), with which an aircraft's

Chapter Four

The *GlobalEye* aircraft during flight test, with the distinctive radar fairing mounted atop the fuselage

position (based on GPS location data) is broadcast via a digital data link either directly to a ground station or via a satellite. The aircraft's mission system can also be configured to work with a number of military-standard data links, depending on which ones are employed by the operating air force. The *GlobalEye* is also fitted with an ESM suite, which is pod-mounted on the aircraft wingtips. This provides 360-degree coverage and gives the ability to detect radar emissions from aircraft, surface ships or ground-based air defences. The received signal is then compared with a threat library to categorise and possibly identify the emitter. In dealing with frequency-agile radar – which is by its very nature harder to identify – the ESM is designed to look for patterns of activity: for instance, whether the emitter pattern resembles that of a maritime-navigation radar or the search radar for a SAM system.

As of the third quarter of 2019, two *GlobalEye* Multi Role Sensor Systems (MRSS) were in flight test and evaluation. The prototype was flown for the first time on 14 March 2018,[65] and has since early September 2018 been based in Granada, Spain. (The weather in Spain is generally more conducive to flight-testing than the occasionally inclement climate of Sweden.) The modification to the airframe, most notably the large upper fuselage canoe, requires that the aircraft's aerodynamic characteristics be fully explored for certification. In the *GlobalEye* configuration, the *Global* 6000-based aircraft has an operational ceiling of 50,000 ft (15,240 m) and an endurance of more than 11 hours.

Project Dolphin
Alongside the acquisition of the *GlobalEye*, the UAE is also bringing into service two multi-sensor SIGINT aircraft under what is known as Project Dolphin, although as with many SIGINT projects, there is comparatively little information about the project in the public domain.[66] (The origins of the UAE requirement likely extend back over a decade.)

The project appears to have had a chequered history, with overall industry responsibility for the project shifting at least once. Two unmodified aircraft were delivered to Marshall in 2012, but issues with the originally proposed mission-system suite delayed progress.[67] A SIGINT system from British-based defence company QinetiQ has since been used as the basis for the programme. The UK's Marshall Defence and Aerospace Group was responsible for the airframe modification, including fitting a long canoe sensor-housing under the forward fuselage, while the aircraft also has a large number of antennae. Ventral strakes are fitted on the rear fuselage to counter the aerodynamic effect of the sensor canoe. A cooling intake positioned ahead of the port-side engine supports the on-board mission equipment. A large conformal satellite-communications antenna is fitted on the upper fuselage.

One of the UAE's modified Project Dolphin SIGINT aircraft prior to being painted

The QinetiQ AS-5 COMINT system is key to the aircraft's role.[68] The AS-5 is described by the company as intended for 'strategic airborne applications' that are able to 'intercept high volumes of signals traffic over a vast operational area'.[69] (The UK's *Rivet Joint* aircraft may also be fitted with the AS-5 as part of its mission-system suite.) The under-fuselage canoe may house a long-range oblique photography system, possibly a variant of the DB-110, which would provide the aircraft also with a capable imagery-gathering system.

The prototype aircraft was flown for the first time on 21 June 2017, with flight tests continuing into 2018. The second aircraft was flown on 8 August 2018. The first of two *Global* 6000-based aircraft was identified being flown from Al Dhafra in early August 2019. The two aircraft will provide a COMINT capability broadly similar to the RSAF's RE-3 when they enter service with the UAE Air Force, giving the UAE the ability to monitor and exploit the communications of state and non-state actors, with Iran of obvious interest.

Recent operations involving ISR

The GCC's ISR capabilities, and limitations, have been foregrounded by the Saudi-led intervention in Yemen's civil war. The region has also provided a crucible in which Russia has found considerable gaps in its own ISR, particularly at the tactical level, in its support for the Assad regime in Syria.

Saudi Arabia and the UAE are the two best-equipped air forces in the GCC. They will be joined by Qatar over the coming years as it introduces into service the Dassault *Rafale*, the Eurofighter *Typhoon* and the F-15QA.[70] This air power was at the fore when on 26 March 2015 Saudi Arabia launched *Operation Decisive Storm*, its intervention in the Yemeni civil war that was aimed at the destruction of the rebels' ground-based air defences and heavy weaponry. Saudi Arabia led a coalition that included all of the other GCC states (except Oman) along with Egypt, Jordan, Morocco, Senegal and Sudan. Up to 100 RSAF aircraft were involved in the initial operation, while the UAE reportedly contributed 30 aircraft,[71] with 15 each from Bahrain and Kuwait and ten from Qatar. *Operation Decisive Storm* was replaced on 22 April 2015 by *Operation Restoring Hope*, which was meant to focus more on a political solution, backed up by the armed forces. As of yet, however, the Saudi Arabia-led intervention has not resulted in a decisive outcome and the civil war in Yemen has continued, while the humanitarian situation in the country has grown increasingly desperate.[72]

RSAF combat aircraft involved in the Yemen operation have included the F-15SA, *Tornado* and *Typhoon*, while the RE-3 and *King Air* 350s have also been involved. The F-15SA has almost certainly been used with the DB-110 reconnaissance pod, while the CH-4 armed UAV has also been employed. The UAE contribution involved the F-16E/F and also the *Mirage* 2000. Its *Wing Loong* and *Predator* XP UAVs have also been used. (In addition, the UAE has reportedly been using its air force in Libya in support of the Libyan National Army.)

The effective use of air power in Yemen, including the provision and use of adequate ISR, has proved a challenge for Saudi Arabia and its allies. The Saudi Arabian intervention has shown areas where the performance of its air force and those of some of its allies has on occasion fallen short of the most experienced of Western forces, such as the US, despite the Saudi-led coalition's use of modern combat aircraft and weapons, together with support from the US.

Given the comparative lack of combat experience of most of the air forces involved and the challenges of the

Chapter Four

RSAF *Typhoon* multi-role fighters have been one of the types involved in the war in Yemen

kind of war being waged in Yemen, this was not necessarily surprising, but shortfalls in the performance of the coalition has had problematic consequences. Shortcomings in ISR and the resulting errors in targeting have contributed to the political difficulties stemming from the intervention, particularly where airstrikes have caused civilian deaths.

In response to political concern over disproportionate civilian casualties as a result of airstrikes, Saudi Arabia led the establishment of the Joint Incidents Assessment Team (JIAT) in May 2016, with members drawn from the coalition. The JIAT is meant to investigate civil casualties resulting from airstrikes, and has on occasion recognised that errors were made. Most notably this included an airstrike in August 2018 on a bus that resulted in the deaths of at least 40 civilians, many of them likely children.

The August 2018 report by the United Nations Group of Experts into the human-rights situation in Yemen claimed that 'coalition air strikes have caused most of the documented civilian casualties'.[73] The report contended that even with an inventory of advanced combat aircraft, the associated air-to-surface weaponry and targeting systems, there was no substitute for appropriate training supported by a rigorous target-selection and approvals process to help minimise civilian casualties:

> Reliable information indicates the Saudi military is trained for conventional state on state conflict, and in particular, to attack military columns in austere environments, and has little if no training relevant to combatting insurgents in urban environments. The type of conventional warfare that the Saudi military is trained to fight would require a different approach to proportionality assessments and precautionary measures from that required when planning military operations in populated areas.[74]

The use of air power in a built-up environment is one of the most difficult kinds of military operations, one where even the US is not immune from making errors, with lethal consequences. Target-location error and a failure of procedure were the root causes of an attack by a USAF AC-130 gunship that killed 42 civilians at a Médecins Sans Frontières hospital in Afghanistan in October 2015.[75]

Political discomfort caused by civilian deaths in Yemen resulting from the air campaign led US politicians to try to block the sale of weapons to Saudi Arabia, the UAE and Jordan in the first half of 2019, but Trump vetoed the proposal.[76] The weapons orders were in part intended to replenish stocks of guided munitions, which had been depleted as a result of the intervention in Yemen. In the UK, the Court of Appeal ruled in June 2019 that the government had not adequately assessed the risk to civilians in approving weapons sales to Saudi Arabia.[77] In July, the British government appealed the decision.[78] Irrespective of the final outcome of the deliberations, the debate highlights the sensitivity of the issue in British political circles.

Part of the challenge for the RSAF and its allies has been the shift in emphasis from deliberate to dynamic targeting. In part, this was inevitable as the number of fixed targets dwindled and combat operations on the ground grew in intensity. Efforts have been made to tighten up the dynamic targeting-approvals process, with officers of greater seniority required to give clearance for a strike than was previously the case.[79]

The relative accuracy of Western air campaigns and their comparative success in avoiding non-combatant deaths in recent wars means that the Western public now has an expectation of precision targeting, almost regardless of the nations engaged in airstrikes. The Western capability, however, is built on three decades of combat experience, experience that none of the participants in the Yemeni air campaign can draw upon.

Russian ISR in Syria

In the latter part of the Soviet era, the Soviet armed forces had a range of ISR UAVs in service and in development, but the collapse of the Soviet Union and subsequent economic turmoil in the 1990s saw Russia fall behind in this area. Over the past decade, however, Russia has invested once again in UAVs, though its domestically designed medium and large UAVs remain in development.

Russia's intervention in Syria in support of the regime of President Bashar al-Assad has provided the Russian armed forces with the opportunity to test a range of new and upgraded systems in combat, including a number of ISR systems and platforms, both crewed and uninhabited. The Russian Air Force's Ilyushin Il-20 *Coot-A* ISR aircraft has been operated from Russia's Hmeimim Air Base in Syria alongside tactical combat aircraft.[80] The Il-20 is used for radar ground surveillance, SIGINT and photo-reconnaissance. The aircraft is fitted with the Leninets *Igla-1* side-looking radar mounted in a housing under the forward fuselage. The aircraft also carries two oblique photography cameras, one on each side of the forward fuselage. Two ELINT systems, *Romb* and *Kvadrat*, are used to gather data on threat radars. The aircraft is also equipped with the *Vishnya* COMINT system. At least some of the *Coot-A* aircraft were upgraded earlier in the decade, but the details of the modifications are not known.[81]

On 17 September 2018, a Russian Air Force Il-20 was mistakenly shot down by Syrian air-defence forces using an S-200 (SA-5 *Gammon*). The Syrian air-defence personnel appeared to believe they were engaging Israeli F-16s that were also operating in the same area as the Il-20.

The air force has also tested the Tupolev Tu-214R ISR aircraft in Syria. The first of the two Tu-214R so far built was flown in July 2008. The aircraft began being operated from Hmeimim in February 2016. Like the *Coot-A*, the aircraft is fitted with a ground-mapping radar/moving-target indicator, SIGINT and the Fraktsiya electro-optical system. The Fraktsiya can produce high-resolution photographs and video in multiple infrared and visible wavelengths and visible-spectrum ranges in real time. The Tu-214R radar system is claimed to be able to penetrate foliage and detect camouflaged targets.[82] It is capable of detecting ballistic missiles at a distance of up to 800 km, bombers within a radius of 650 km, and fighter jets at a distance of up to 300 km.

The A-50U *Mainstay* AEW&C aircraft has also been deployed to Hmeimim at various stages during Russia's involvement in Syria. The aircraft was reported to be in Syria in late 2015, but appeared to have returned to Russia in the second quarter of 2016. By May 2017, the A-50U was again deployed in Syria.[83]

Russian UAVs in Syria

Russia has made widespread use of UAVs in operations in Syria. In February 2016, the Russian Ministry of Defence said that around 70 UAVs had been deployed.[84] Types deployed have included the *Eleron-3SV*, the *Takhion*, the *Orlan-10*, the *Granat-4* and the *Forpost*. One of the main uses of UAVs in Syria was carrying out reconnaissance in support of airstrikes,[85] battle-damage assessment and in the adjustment of artillery fire.

The *Eleron-3SV*, first procured in 2013, is one of the lightest UAVs used by the Russian military in Syria. The UAV weighs 4.3 kg (without payload), has a 1.4 m span and is powered by a low-noise electric motor, resulting in a very small acoustic signature. The *Eleron* has a two-hour endurance and can be data-linked at a range of up to 25 km from the ground station. The use of the *Eleron* in Syria became apparent following the loss of a UAV in territory held by opposition forces in mid-2015, before the official start of Russia's military operation in Syria.[86]

The *Takhion* is another small electric-powered UAV used by Russia in Syria. The *Takhion* entered service with the Russian armed forces at the end of 2014, and like the *Eleron* is a flying-wing design. The maximum weight of the *Takhion* is 7 kg, and it can be fitted with a video camera or thermal imager. It can be operated at a range of up to 40 km and has a two-hour endurance.

The *Orlan-10* is possibly the most numerous Russian UAV employed in Syria. This UAV has a take-off weight of between 16 kg and 18 kg and can carry a 5 kg payload. It is powered by a small piston engine. It has an endurance of 16 hours and has an operational range of up to 100 km. These UAVs have also been used for mapping, convoy escort and search-and-rescue operations. The surviving crew member of the Sukhoi Su-24M2 *Fencer* shot down by the Turkish Air Force was located using an *Orlan-10*.[87]

Chapter Four

The *Granat-4* is a slightly larger UAV used by Russian forces in Syria.[88] Like the *Orlan-10*, it uses a piston engine. The *Granat-4* has a maximum take-off weight of 30 kg and an operational range of 70 km. Payloads of up to 3 kg can be carried, including EO and COMINT systems.

The largest and most capable of the Russian UAVs so far deployed is the *Forpost*, a licence-built Israeli *Searcher*. These have predominantly been used to support airstrikes on high-priority targets. While units with light UAVs have been deployed across Syria, *Forpost* UAVs were located at Hmeimim, Aleppo airport and the T-4 Air Base near Palmyra, Homs governorate. The *Forpost* was deployed to observe the first use of the 3M14 (SS-N-30A) land-attack missiles fired from the submarine *Rostov-on-Don* in the Mediterranean Sea on 8 December 2015, and the three targets that were struck.[89]

The lessons on offer from Russia's use of ISR in Syria are informing Moscow's domestic programmes, not least in the renewed emphasis on the development of a broad range of UAVs capable of providing ISR at the tactical and operational levels.

Notes

1 US Central Command, 'Combined Air Operations Center', 1 July 2017, https://www.afcent.af.mil/About/Fact-Sheets/Display/Article/217803/combined-air-operations-center-caoc/.

2 Rachel S. Cohen, 'Offutt's ISR Planes Prep for Evolving Threats', *Air Force Magazine*, July/August 2019, pp. 19–20, http://www.airforcemag.com/MagazineArchive/Magazine%20Documents/2019/July%202019/AFM_July-August%202019%20Full%20Issue.pdf.

3 Melissa Leon and Jennifer Griffin, 'Pentagon "Very Carefully Watching China", it's "No. 1 Priority", Defense Secretary Mark Esper tells Fox News', Fox News, 22 August 2019, https://www.foxnews.com/politics/pentagon-china-defense-secretary-mark-esper.

4 John Vandiver, 'EUCOM Commander Requests Two More Destroyers, Extra Ground Troops for Europe', *Stars and Stripes*, 5 March 2019, https://www.stripes.com/news/eucom-commander-requests-two-more-navy-destroyers-extra-ground-troops-for-europe-1.571427.

5 Chris Pocock, *Dragon Lady Today: The Continuing Story of the U-2 Spyplane* (Scotts Valley, CA: CreateSpace Independent Publishing Platform, 2014), various pages.

6 *Ibid.*, pp. 25–33.

7 *Ibid.*

8 US Naval War College, 'Intelligence Studies: Types of Intelligence Collection', https://usnwc.libguides.com/c.php?g=494120&p=3381426.

9 Pocock, *Dragon Lady Today*, pp. 34–5, and General James Mattis's testimony to US House of Representatives' Armed Services Committee, 6 March 2012.

10 Pocock, *Dragon Lady Today*, pp. 30–1.

11 Federation of American Scientists, 'National Image Interpretability Ratings Scales', 16 January 1998, https://fas.org/irp/imint/niirs.htm.

12 *Ibid.*

13 Melissa Dalton and Hijab Shah, 'U.S. Support for Saudi Military Operations in Yemen', Center for Strategic and International Studies, 23 March 2018, https://www.csis.org/analysis/us-support-saudi-military-operations-yemen.

14 Various UK Foreign Office cables made public by WikiLeaks.

15 Martin Streetly, 'The New Face of Airborne SIGINT: Global, Civil and in Real Time', *International Defence Review*, 30 November 2010, https://janes.ihs.com/Janes/Display/idr13578-idr-2011.

16 Scarlet Kim and Paulina Perlin, 'Newly Disclosed NSA Documents Shed Further Light on Five Eyes Alliance', Lawfare blog, 25 March 2019, https://www.lawfareblog.com/newly-disclosed-nsa-documents-shed-further-light-five-eyes-alliance.

17 Jeremy Binnie, 'Analysis, Iran Unveils Bavar-373 for a Second Time', *Jane's Defence Weekly*, 23 August 2019, https://janes.ihs.com/Janes/Display/FG_2367742-JDW.

18 US Joint Chiefs of Staff, 'Electronic Warfare', Joint Publication 3-13.1, 8 February 2012, pp. i–17, https://publicintelligence.net/jcs-electronic-warfare/.

19 Marina Malenic, 'Flying High', *Air Force Magazine*, February 2012, http://www.airforcemag.com/MagazineArchive/Pages/2012/February%202012/0212igh.aspx.

20 Various media reports; interview with senior Northrop Grumman official.

21 Northrop Grumman, 'Global Hawk Architecture', 2012, https://www.northropgrumman.com/Capabilities/GlobalHawk/Documents/Brochure_Q4_HALE_Enterprise.pdf.

22 Various media reports; Northrop Grumman press releases.

23 Elizabeth McCann, 'BAMS-D: Still Going Strong', Northrop Grumman magazine *(r)evolution*, July/October 2017, pp. 26–7, https://www.northropgrumman.com/Capabilities/Triton/Documents/pageDocuments/BAMS_D_Still_Going_Strong.pdf.

24 David Martin, Fin Gomez and Camilo Montoya-Galvez, 'Trump Orders Limited Strike on Iran but Then Calls It Off', CBS News, 21 June 2019, https://www.cbsnews.com/news/iran-drone-donald-trump-orders-limited-strike-but-calls-it-off-unknown-reasons-live-updates-2019-06-21/.

25 Northrop Grumman, 'Global Hawk Architecture'.

26 Joseph Trevithick, 'USAF Plans to Drastically Boost Flexibility of U-2s and RQ-4s By Adding Modular "Agile Pods", The Drive, 10 September 2018, https://www.thedrive.com/the-war-zone/23489/usaf-plans-to-drastically-boost-flexibility-of-u-2s-and-rq-4s-by-adding-modular-agile-pods.

27 Northrop Grumman, 'Global Hawk Architecture'.

28 Jeremy Binnie, 'IDEX 2013: UAE Orders Predator XP', *Jane's Defence Weekly*, 20 February 2013, https://janes.ihs.com/Janes/Display/jdw51408-jdw-2013.

29 Noah Shachtman, 'Is This the Secret U.S. Drone Base in Saudi Arabia?', *Wired*, 7 February 2013, https://www.wired.com/2013/02/secret-drone-base-2/.

30 US Central Command, 'Statement from US Central Command Statement on Attacks Against US Observation Aircraft', 16 June 2019, https://www.centcom.mil/media/statements/statements-view/article/1877252/statement-from-us-central-command-on-attacks-against-us-observation-aircraft/.

31 Gareth Jennings, 'DoD Contracts DB-110 Recon Pods for Middle East Air Forces', *Jane's Defence Weekly*, 28 February 2019, https://www.janes.com/article/86925/dod-contracts-db-110-recon-pods-for-middle-east-air-forces.

32 UTC Aerospace Systems (UTAS), 'Beyond Horizons: A Unique Partnership Between the RAF and UTC Aerospace Systems' booklet, 2016; Collins Aerospace information response, 2019.

33 UTAS, 'Beyond Horizons' booklet.

34 Collins Aerospace information response.

35 *Ibid.*

36 UTAS, 'Beyond Horizons' booklet.

37 David Donald, 'UAE is Launch Customer for Multi-spectral Recon Pod', AINonline, 13 November 2017, https://www.ainonline.com/aviation-news/defense/2017-11-13/uae-launch-customer-multi-spectral-recon-pod.

38 UTAS, 'Beyond Horizons' booklet.

39 *Ibid.*; Collins Aerospace information response.

40 UTAS, 'Beyond Horizons' booklet; Chris Pockock, 'UTC Wins New Customers For DB- and MS-110 Sensor', 21 February 2018, https://www.ainonline.com/aviation-news/defense/2018-02-21/utc-wins-new-customers-db-and-ms-110-sensor.

41 Collins Aerospace information response; unofficial source.

42 UTAS, 'Beyond Horizons' booklet; multiple unofficial open sources.

43 Jeremy Binnie, 'Saudis Request King Air ISR Aircraft', *Jane's Defence Weekly*, 17 August 2012, https://janes.ihs.com/Janes/Display/jdw49873-jdw-2012.

44 dafeng cao (@dafengcao), 'It's unveiled in the National Sci & Tech Progress Award …', 15 February 2018, Tweet, https://twitter.com/search?q=CH-4%20Saudi&src=typed_query.

45 Caleb Henry, 'Airbus Defence and Space Awarded Falcon Eye Contract by UAE Military', Satellite Today, 9 December 2014, https://www.satellitetoday.com/government-military/2014/12/09/airbus-defence-and-space-awarded-falcon-eye-contract-by-uae-military/.

46 UAE Space Agency, 'The UAE Space Sector', April 2018, https://www.sasic.sa.gov.au/docs/default-source/5th-sa-space-forum-presentations/1015---naser-al-hammadi-and-abir-khater.pdf.

47 Cullen Desforges, 'Falcon Eye 1 Lost in Vega Launcher Mishap', Spaceflight Insider, 10 July 2019, https://www.spaceflightinsider.com/organizations/esa/falcon-eye-1-spacecraft-lost-in-vega-mishap/.

48 Chris Bergen, 'Vega Suffers her First Failure During Falcon Eye-1 Launch', NASA Spaceflight.com, 10 July 2019, https://www.nasaspaceflight.com/2019/07/vega-suffers-her-first-failure-during-falcon-eye-1-launch/.

49 Doug Messier, 'An Overview of UAE Space Agency', Parabolic Arc, 26 May 2015, http://www.parabolicarc.com/2015/05/26/over-view-uae-space-agency/.

50 Sam Bridge, 'King Announces Plans to Set Up Saudi Space Agency', Arabian Business, 28 December 2018, https://www.arabianbusiness.com/technology/410411-plans-revealed-to-set-up-saudi-space-agency.

51 Sarwat Nasir, 'UAE Launches Arab Space Collaboration Group', *Khaleej Times*, 19 March 2019, https://www.khaleejtimes.com/uae-launches-arab-space-collaboration-group.

52 Kelvin Wong, 'China's CASC Quietly Rolls Out AR-1B Precision Missile', *Jane's International Defence Review*, 13 November 2018, https://janes.ihs.com/Janes/Display/FG_1268812-IDR.

53 Kelvin Wong, 'CASC Showcases New Generation of UAV Weapons', *Jane's International Defence Review*, 20 November 2014, https://janes.ihs.com/Janes/Display/idr17186-idr-2014.

54 Peter Felstead, 'Farnborough 2018: Initial UAE GlobalEye Delivery Likely by End of Year', *Jane's Defence Weekly*, 18 July 2018, https://janes.ihs.com/Janes/Display/FG_975653-JDW.

55 Mark Kwiatkowski, 'Project Dolphin Surfaces with UAE Air Force Markings', FlightGlobal, 24 August 2018, https://www.flightglobal.com/news/articles/picture-project-dolphin-surfaces-with-uae-air-force-451373/.

56 Richard D. Fisher Jr, 'IDEX 2015: Blue Arrow 9 Further Expands Chinese UAV Weapon Options', *Jane's Defence Weekly*, 25 February 2015, https://janes.ihs.com/Janes/Display/jdw57872-jdw-2015.

57 'Turkey Prepares to Deliver "Bayraktar TB2" Drones to Qatar', *Peninsula*, 9 February 2019, https://thepeninsulaqatar.com/article/09/02/2019/Turkey-prepares-to-deliver-Bayraktar-TB2-drones-to-Qatar.

58 Angus Batey, 'UAE, Saab Strike $1.27 Billion Erieye Deal', *Aviation Week*, 10 November 2015, https://aviationweek.com/dubai-air-show-2015/uae-saab-strike-127-billion-erieye-deal.

59 *Ibid.*

60 Craig Hoyle, 'Saab CEO Confirms Order for Third GlobalEye Aircraft', FlightGlobal, 26 April 2017, https://www.flightglobal.com/news/articles/saab-ceo-confirms-order-for-third-globaleye-aircraft-436590/.

61 See IISS, *The Military Balance 2019* (Abingdon: Routledge for the IISS, 2019), p. 366.

62 Craig Hoyle, 'Dubai 09: UAE Signs for Two Saab 340-based Early Warning Aircraft', FlightGlobal, 17 November 2009, https://www.flightglobal.com/news/articles/dubai-09-uae-signs-for-two-saab-340-based-early-war-335116/.

63 Saab, 'Redefining the Airborne Surveillance Market', press

Chapter Four

briefing, slide 11, https://saabgroup.com/globalassets/cision/documents/2016/pressbrief-singapore-globaleye.pdf.

64 *Ibid.*

65 'Successful First Flight for GlobalEye', Saab press release, 14 March 2018, https://saabgroup.com/media/news-press/news/2018-03/successful-first-flight-for-globaleye/.

66 Tony Osborne, 'Intrigue Surrounds Heavily Modified Global Business Jet', *Aviation Week & Space Technology*, 5 May 2017, https://aviationweek.com/intelligence-surveillance-reconnaissance/intrigue-surrounds-heavily-modified-global-business-jet.

67 Alan Warnes, 'High Spy. But Will the UAE Spy Planes Be Up to the Challenge?', Arabian Aerospace, 8 November 2018, https://www.arabianaerospace.aero/high-spy-but-will-the-uae-spy-planes-be-up-to-the-challenge-.html.

68 *Ibid.*

69 QinetiQ, 'Electronic Surveillance', https://www.qinetiq.com/what-we-do/c4isr/electronic-surveillance.

70 Gareth Jennings, 'Parting Shot: Qatar Emiri Air Force Fighter Procurement', *Jane's International Defence Review*, 11 January 2018, https://janes.ihs.com/Janes/Display/FG_714262-IDR.

71 Michael Knights and Alexander Mello, 'The Saudi-UAE War Effort in Yemen (Part 2): The Air Campaign', Washington Institute, 11 August 2015, https://www.washingtoninstitute.org/policy-analysis/view/the-saudi-uae-war-effort-in-yemen-part-2-the-air-campaign.

72 Nabih Bulos and David S. Cloud, 'As Top Allies Scale Back in Yemen, Saudi Arabia Faces Prospect of an Unwinnable War', *Los Angeles Times*, 11 August 2019, https://www.latimes.com/world-nation/story/2019-08-11/yemen-saudi-arabia-face-unwinnable-war.

73 UN High Commissioner for Human Rights, 'Situation of Human Rights in Yemen, Including Violations and Abuses since September 2014', A/HRC/39/43, 17 August 2018, p. 5, https://reliefweb.int/sites/reliefweb.int/files/resources/A_HRC_39_43_EN.pdf.

74 *Ibid.*, pp. 36–7.

75 Médecins Sans Frontières, 'Kunduz Hospital Attack', https://www.msf.org/kunduz-hospital-attack.

76 Joe Gould, 'Trump Vetoes Congressional Action to Block Saudi Arms Sales', *Defense News*, 24 July 2019, https://www.defensenews.com/congress/2019/07/25/trump-vetoes-congressional-action-to-block-saudi-arms-sales/.

77 Dan Sabbagh and Bethan McKernan, 'UK Arms Sales to Saudi Arabia Unlawful, Court of Appeal Declares', *Guardian*, 20 June 2019, https://www.theguardian.com/law/2019/jun/20/uk-arms-sales-to-saudi-arabia-for-use-in-yemen-declared-unlawful.

78 Dan Sabbagh, 'UK Ministers Challenge UK Court Ruling on Saudi Arabia Arms Sales', *Guardian*, 8 July 2019, https://www.theguardian.com/politics/2019/jul/08/uk-ministers-challenge-court-ruling-on-saudi-arabia-arms-sales.

79 Jeremy Binnie, 'UK Sees Improved Saudi Targeting in Yemen', *Jane's Defence Weekly*, 12 July 2017, https://janes.ihs.com/Janes/Display/FG_551418-JDW.

80 'Ил-20' [IL-20], Airwar.ru, http://www.airwar.ru/enc/spy/il20.html.

81 EME's annual reports, V.M. Myasishchev, 2010–12, http://www.emz-m.ru/?id=41.

82 'Новый российский самолет-разведчик научили «видеть» подземные объекты' [The New Russian Reconnaissance Aircraft Taught to 'See' Underground Objects], vz.ru, 8 June 2015, https://vz.ru/news/2015/6/8/749644.html.

83 Barbara Opall-Rome, 'Satellite Imagery Shows Russian AWACS Back in Syria', *Defense News*, 7 May 2017, https://www.defensenews.com/global/mideast-africa/2017/05/07/satellite-imagery-shows-russian-awacs-back-in-syria/.

84 'Минобороны РФ: контроль в Сирии ведут с применением 70 беспилотников' [Russian Defense Ministry: Control in Syria Using 70 Drones], RIA Novosti, 27 February 2016, https://ria.ru/20160227/1381173504.html?in=t.

85 A.A. Turik, V.I. Miroshnikov and S.A. Goncharov, Применение БПЛА сторонами при ведении боевых действий в САР [Use of UAVs by the Parties in the Conduct of Hostilities in the ATS], Russian Drone, 3 October 2018, https://russiandrone.ru/publications/primenenie-bpla-storonami-pri-vedenii-boevykh-deystviy-v-sar/.

86 'Russian «Eleron-3SV» UAV lost over Syria', Defence Blog, 21 July 2015, https://defence-blog.com/news/russian-eleron-3sv-lost-over-syria.html.

87 Turik, Miroshnikov and Goncharov, 'Use of UAVs by Parties in the Conduct of Hostilities in the ATS'.

88 'КОМПЛЕКС ДИСТАНЦИОННОГО НАБЛЮДЕНИЯ И РЕТРАНСЛЯЦИИ «ГРАНАТ-4»' [Granat-4 Remote Surveillance and Relay Complex], Nevskii Bastion, 22 October 2015, http://nevskii-bastion.ru/granat-4/.

89 Anton Lavrov, 'Опыт боевого применения российских беспилотных летательных аппаратов в Сирии' [Experience of Combat Use of Russian Drones in Syria], BMPD blog, 4 May 2017, https://bmpd.livejournal.com/2587680.html.

Chapter Five

Maritime ISR

The Gulf and the Strait of Hormuz represent the classic case of a confined, constrained, cluttered, contested and connected maritime environment, and pose a significant maritime intelligence, surveillance and reconnaissance (ISR) challenge.

The Gulf extends to some 241,000 square kilometres, is nearly 1,000 km in length and approximately 340 km across at its widest point. There are thousands of shipping movements of some description around the Gulf every day, with one estimate putting the number of cargo-carrying ship movements through the Strait of Hormuz at more than 67,000 in 2018, or 185 a day on average.[1] In addition to the mushrooming of bulk carrier traffic brought on by the energy trade, there has been a compounding increase in traffic as a result of increased per capita income among Gulf Arab states and therefore of Gulf spending.

Due to its special geostrategic characteristics, the Strait of Hormuz has most regularly grabbed the global headlines. Of all the global maritime choke points – those eight or so[2] key narrows through which passes the vast bulk of maritime trade (itself more than 80% by volume of all global trade) – the Strait of Hormuz is the most critical maritime conduit for energy trade, accounting for 30% of all crude oil and other liquids traded by sea.[3] The strait is only 34 km wide at its narrowest point, with one shipping lane in each direction (each 3.2 km wide) and a buffer zone in between, but is deep enough for the passage of the world's largest crude-oil and natural-gas carriers. Notwithstanding the recent prominence of frictions in and around the South China Sea, the Strait of Hormuz has been the arena in which issues of freedom of navigation and protection of sea lines of communication (SLOCs) have been most tested and contested.

In addition to the complexity and density of maritime trade, the Gulf and the Strait of Hormuz lie in a region that has faced considerable political turmoil for much of the past four decades. The Western maritime-security posture over that period focused on countering Iranian influence in the waterways, a posture that has become more diffi-

Smoke pours out of the Norwegian-owned *Front Altair* tanker on 13 June 2019 after it was damaged by an explosion in the Gulf of Oman

ISR & the Gulf: An Assessment

Chapter Five

cult in the face of recent events. The increasing number of 'grey-zone' incidents (i.e., confrontations that fall short of armed conflict) in and around the Strait of Hormuz during 2019 – the Iranian response to the US withdrawal from the Joint Comprehensive Plan of Action (JCPOA) and the application of the Trump administration's 'maximum pressure' policy towards Iran, including renewed sanctions – has challenged certain assumptions about the provision of maritime security in the region, as well as what is enduring and what is novel about the challenges to that security. This situation has posed new questions about the kinds of capabilities required, not least in the area of maritime ISR.

Troubled waters

From a maritime-security point of view, for much of the twentieth century the Gulf was essentially first a British and latterly a United States area of influence. Historically, the naval and maritime capabilities of the Gulf Arab states were limited. The US was initially reluctant to take on the maritime-security responsibilities of the erstwhile leading maritime power in the region (the United Kingdom), maintaining only a relatively limited presence during the 1970s.

The character of the maritime-security architecture in the region, and the regional geostrategic environment more broadly, changed dramatically in 1979 with the Soviet invasion of Afghanistan and the Islamic Revolution in Iran, which suddenly increased the perceived strategic vulnerability for US interests. The new strategic situation was characterised by the combination of the antagonism between the US and Iran, regional frictions and confrontation, and the strategic importance of the Gulf. The US naval presence grew and was eventually consolidated under a reactivated US Navy Fifth Fleet in 1995, headquartered in Bahrain at what had been for some time the US Navy's main administrative shore facility in the region.

Maritime tensions increased during the Iran–Iraq War from 1980–88, highlighting the vital importance of effective maritime ISR in the region. The Tanker War reached its height in 1987–88 after Iraq escalated its attacks on Iranian oil exports and Iran, which had successfully blockaded Iraqi Gulf oil exports and had bottled up the Iraqi Navy, increased its attacks on shipping and oil infrastructure belonging to Iraq's chief Gulf Arab supporters.[4]

In July 1987, the US launched *Operation Earnest Will*, escorting Kuwaiti oil tankers reflagged to the US. As an indicator perhaps of a lack of preparedness by the US Navy and a lack of sufficient ISR, or at least a failure to act on intelligence, a tanker in the very first convoy, the reflagged vessel *Bridgeton*, was damaged by a mine. In the immediate aftermath of this, the US launched a covert mission using helicopters and patrol boats operating principally from two leased barges in the northern Gulf to monitor and counter Iranian mining operations.

In August 1987, US forces detected the Iranian vessel *Iran Ajr* covertly laying mines, and attacked and captured the vessel. In April 1988, the frigate USS *Samuel B. Roberts* was struck and badly damaged by a mine. Within days, US naval forces launched *Operation Praying Mantis*, sinking an Iranian frigate and putting a significant part of Iran's conventional naval capability out of action.[5] One of the lessons of this confrontation for Iran was the vulnerability of its conventional naval capabilities in the face of US-led forces, reinforcing Iran's increasing focus on an asymmetric force structure.

One further major incident during this period was the downing of Iran Air Flight 655 on 3 July 1988 by the US Navy cruiser USS *Vincennes*, with the loss of all 290 passengers and crew. The US vessel misidentified the civilian airliner as an attacking Iranian F-14 fighter. The incident was the subject of enormous controversy,[6] and in part may have been caused by the lack of a clear maritime

Reflagged tankers being escorted by US warships near the coast of Dubai on 18 January 1988

The International Institute for Strategic Studies

Maritime ISR

The captured Iranian mine-laying ship *Iran Ajr* with a US Navy landing craft alongside, 22 September 1987

and air picture. The incident is also likely to have been a significant contributory factor in Iran later that month accepting a ceasefire in the long-running conflict.

After the end of the Iran–Iraq War, the waterways of the Gulf and the Strait of Hormuz continued to witness significant maritime tensions and activity. In 1991, US and coalition naval forces were heavily involved in *Operation Desert Storm* to expel occupying Iraqi forces from Kuwait, including destroying much of the Iraqi Navy. US and UK naval forces also supported enforcement of the southern no-fly zone over Iraq during the 1990s. US, UK and Australian naval forces also took part in the early stages of the US-led invasion of Iraq in 2003.

Meanwhile, the waters continued to be a focus of ebbs and flows in tensions with Iran, particularly in 2008–09 and again in 2011–12, as Tehran issued periodic threats to close the Strait of Hormuz as part of the long-running stand-off over its suspected nuclear-weapons ambitions. A spike in incidents involving the harassment of US Navy vessels by Iran's Islamic Revolutionary Guard Corps Navy (IRGCN) boats in 2016 prompted the then US chief of naval operations Admiral John Richardson to warn of a 'new normal' in terms of such potential encounters and flashpoints at sea.[7] While frictions in fact subsided somewhat for a time after 2016, the increase in incidents during 2019 in the Strait of Hormuz has underscored the fact that the waterway and potential threats to it remain a central hub of Tehran's coercive or deterrent 'defence diplomacy', and the tap which Iran turns on and off to raise or lower the diplomatic temperature.

The escalation of the conflict in Yemen also introduced a further maritime-security concern, with an apparent increased threat to maritime traffic in the Bab el-Mandeb Strait and the southern Red Sea, as well as the use of maritime routes to smuggle weaponry and supplies to Ansarullah rebel forces – also known as the Houthis. In October 2016, Houthi rebels launched two attacks – one successfully against a high-speed supply vessel operated by the United Arab Emirates (UAE) and apparently one

The Iranian navy conducts the *Velayat*-90 naval exercises on 1 January 2012 in the Strait of Hormuz

ISR & the Gulf: An Assessment

81

Chapter Five

unsuccessfully against a US warship – using anti-ship missiles that were widely assumed to have been supplied by Iran, raising the spectre of the further proliferation of such capabilities, including to non-state actors. This may also raise the bar in terms of the capabilities required to protect against such threats, particularly in narrow waterways and the complex and congested littorals, including the Strait of Hormuz and the Gulf.[8]

The challenge to US and Western ISR in the Gulf

The aim of maritime domain awareness is to be able to produce a recognised maritime picture (RMP): to not only locate but also to identify and, if needed, prosecute potential targets.

As stated in the US Navy's Maritime Domain Awareness Concept (made public in 2007), the US prioritised the achievement of maritime domain awareness driven by an increased focus on littoral operations. As the US Navy saw it, the picture was getting dramatically more complicated, the number of organic ISR assets directly available to deployed naval forces was dwindling and yet the inflow of information was proving beyond the ability of the analysts to process.

While the littoral arena has become increasingly problematic, the blue-water requirement has also returned with a vengeance due to the revival of great-power competition, particularly as far as the US national-defence strategy is concerned. On top of that, there is a techno-

Gulf maritime tensions rise: May–September 2019

5 May
The US announces the deployment of a bomber task force and the accelerated deployment of the USS *Abraham Lincoln* Carrier Strike Group to the Gulf region in response to an escalation of tensions with Iran.

12–13 May
Four oil tankers (two Saudi, one Emirati and one Norwegian) are damaged by explosions in a 'sabotage attack' off the UAE coast in the Gulf of Oman. The United States blames Iran but Tehran denies any involvement.

13 June
A Japanese and a Norwegian tanker suffer explosions while under way in the Gulf of Oman, reportedly the result of limpet mines. The US releases video footage apparently showing Iranian forces removing an unexploded limpet mine from one of the damaged vessels. Iran says the evidence is fabricated.

20 June
Iran shoots down a US Broad Area Maritime Surveillance Demonstrator (BAMS-D) uninhabited aerial vehicle (UAV) just outside the Strait of Hormuz. US President Donald Trump approves, then aborts, US military strikes in response.

4 July
British Royal Marines seize *Grace* 1, an Iranian tanker, near Gibraltar, alleging that the ship's cargo of crude oil was destined for Syria in contravention of a European Union embargo. Iranian officials describe the seizure as 'piracy'.

11 July
British frigate HMS *Montrose* intervenes in the Strait of Hormuz to prevent the apparent attempted interception of the tanker *British Heritage* by three Iranian boats.

13 July
Iran seizes Panamanian-flagged tanker *Riah* near the Strait of Hormuz for 'smuggling fuel'.

18 July
An amphibious assault ship, the USS *Boxer*, downs an Iranian UAV near the Strait of Hormuz.

19 July
The IRGC Navy seizes the *Stena Impero*, a British-flagged tanker, near the Strait of Hormuz. US Central Command announces that it is developing a multinational maritime effort, *Operation Sentinel*, to increase surveillance of and security in key waterways in the Middle East.

22 July
UK foreign secretary Jeremy Hunt announces that the UK is seeking to put together an EU-led maritime security operation for the Gulf.

25 July
The UK government announces that the Royal Navy has been tasked with accompanying UK-flagged ships through the Strait of Hormuz.

28 July
The UK destroyer HMS *Duncan* is deployed to the Gulf, working alongside the frigate HMS *Montrose*. The UK Ministry of Defence announces HMS *Montrose* has accompanied 35 vessels through the Strait of Hormuz.

5 August
The UK announces that it is joining the US-led 'international maritime security construct' for the Gulf. Iranian state media announce the seizure of an Iraqi vessel near Farsi Island for 'smuggling fuel'.

12 August
Frigate HMS *Kent* departs Portsmouth to bolster UK Gulf deployment.

15 August
Iranian tanker *Grace* 1, renamed *Adrian Darya* 1, is released by Gibraltar authorities after Iran pledges that the ship will not transport its cargo of crude oil to Syria, although it is later detected anchored off the coast of Syria in September.

21 August
Australia announces that it will join the US-led maritime security mission.

24 August
The UK government announces that the destroyer HMS *Defender* has been added to the Gulf deployment.

2 September
HMS *Montrose* reports 115 'confrontations' or 'interactions' with the IRGCN in two months. The frigate and HMS *Duncan* accompanied 90 British-flagged vessels totalling nearly 6 million tonnes in that time.

7 September
Frigate HMS *Kent* arrives in the Gulf to relieve HMS *Duncan*.

logical revolution under way, which is placing even more of a premium on information dominance.

This poses a challenge not only for the US Navy but also for its allies and partners in and around the Gulf, given that, as far as great-power competition is concerned, the priority regions lie elsewhere. The alarm bells rang in 2015 when there was a gap in the US Navy aircraft-carrier presence in the Gulf for the first time in eight years. This was played down as a symptom rather than a crisis, and it was a time when Gulf waters were not as choppy as they had been.[9] Nevertheless, it looked like a harbinger, not least perhaps as far as precious ISR assets were concerned.

Since then, the Gulf seemingly got used to periodic 'carrier gaps', with the US on occasion substituting other capabilities such as big-deck amphibious ships with more limited naval-aviation capabilities. But that began to look more problematic again when maritime tensions began to rise in 2019. One US response was to accelerate the next carrier deployment to the region,[10] which could be interpreted as evidence of the inherent flexibility of naval power but might also look like an acknowledgement that US forces are spread thin.

In fact, a carrier presence can represent a mixed blessing in a purely maritime ISR context. Of course, it brings with it its own ISR assets, including the E-2D *Hawkeye* airborne warning and control (AW&C) aircraft and its embarked F/A-18E/F *Super Hornet*, but these tend to be preoccupied with the carrier's own protection rather than being available for more strategic ISR. At the same time, the presence of a carrier tends to draw in other surface combatants that might be otherwise employed independently in ISR tasking. However, the increased use of big-deck amphibious ships as an alternative to a carrier would also bring F-35B *Lightning*s, which have considerable ISR potential.

For now, only the US can deploy the full spectrum of multi-domain platforms required to deliver a comprehensive range of maritime ISR capabilities, from space-based assets to inhabited and uninhabited airborne assets; surface platforms and capabilities such as human-intelligence teams which can provide a surface picture; and sub-surface assets such as electronic and acoustic arrays, which are the surveillance capabilities inherent in submarines and even remote underwater vehicles.

However, it is acknowledged even in the US maritime community that this has to be a multi-agency and even a multinational endeavour, since the US is not strong in all areas, nor does it have unlimited resources. One of those areas of relative US weakness in the Gulf is mine countermeasures (MCM). In this domain, the US is supported by others, such as the UK, but not particularly by the local Gulf Arab states, which also lack such capability.

The diversity of the maritime domain also means that there are commercial assets that can be leveraged, particularly when the priority is lower-end constabulary requirements. The best-known of these is the Automatic Identification System (AIS), a very-high-frequency transceiver system required by the United Nations maritime watchdog, the International Maritime Organization, for all vessels over 300 gross tonnage engaged on interna-

An RQ-21A *Blackjack* UAV preparing for launch from an amphibious transport dock ship, the USS *John P. Murtha*, in the Gulf in July 2019

ISR & the Gulf: An Assessment

Chapter Five

UK Royal Navy *Wildcat* helicopters, like this one, have been deployed in the Gulf

tional voyages; cargo ships of more than 500 gross tonnage operating in local waters; and all passenger vessels. The AIS transmits ship course and speed and other basic identification information. Another such network is the satellite-based Long-Range Identification and Tracking System (LRIT).

Such commercial systems are valuable tools in establishing pattern-of-life movements and help spot anomalies (warships, for example, tend not to display the same regular and predictable tracks as merchant vessels). This is clearly of value in assessing how to respond to 'grey zone' incidents, which are becoming more prevalent including at sea. But even in these situations, AIS and other such systems are vulnerable to 'spoofing'.[11] Such systems are also potentially of greater value to non-state actors that lack access to other ISR capabilities.

What none of the US allies and partners in the region can currently deliver is the high-end persistent or near-persistent overwatch that can provide the more strategic as well as the tactical and local ISR picture. Even a major ally like the UK has been limited in its ability to deliver capability beyond the resources of the few individual surface platforms it has deployed in the region. The UK Royal Navy's main surface combatants can deploy the embarked *Wildcat* helicopter with 360-degree active electronically scanned surveillance radar and electro-optical/forward-looking infrared (FLIR) sight, which represents a considerable ISR capability, but its airborne endurance and therefore time on task is limited.

The UK's approach to deploying maritime ISR assets into the region may change if its new-generation *Queen Elizabeth*-class aircraft carriers are regularly deployed to the Gulf. One potential bonus of these aircraft carriers is that they should bring with them the ISR potential of the F-35B *Lightning* and the UK's other shipborne rotary ISR assets – including the *Crowsnest* AW&C system and *Merlin* and *Wildcat* helicopters in some numbers.

The UK has in the past operated the small *ScanEagle* shipborne uninhabited aerial vehicle (UAV) on operations in the Gulf, and has also done so on counter-piracy missions, as has Canada. However, while the potential for using such shipborne UAVs for ISR has long been recognised by naval forces (indeed the Royal Navy's procuring of the system was in the context of an urgent operational requirement), until recently their adoption has been relatively slow outside the US Navy.[12]

For the US Navy itself, these organic UAV capabilities have already become key elements of its surveillance architecture.[13] The increasing use of UAVs will continue, in part because of the need to compensate for the limited number of inhabited airborne and surface platforms now in global inventories, but the development of maritime ISR in the region will also still need to be multifaceted, given the character of the challenge. In terms of the surface environment alone, a threat scenario is likely to involve a swarm of fast-moving craft against the backdrop of littoral 'clutter' (reflections from land complicating the radar picture) and the likely presence of large numbers of non-combatant vessels, in conditions that will make radar and even electro-optical propagation difficult.

The maritime ISR challenge in the Gulf is further complicated by the potential of competing maritime-security demands of other areas across the region. The regional maritime challenges may oscillate between the Strait of Hormuz, the Bab el-Mandeb Strait and the southern Red Sea, or even arise in all three simultaneously,

A US Department of Defense image reportedly showing the IRGCN after it removed an unexploded limpet mine from the tanker *Kokuka Courageous* in the Gulf of Oman, 13 June 2019

84   The International Institute for Strategic Studies

Maritime ISR

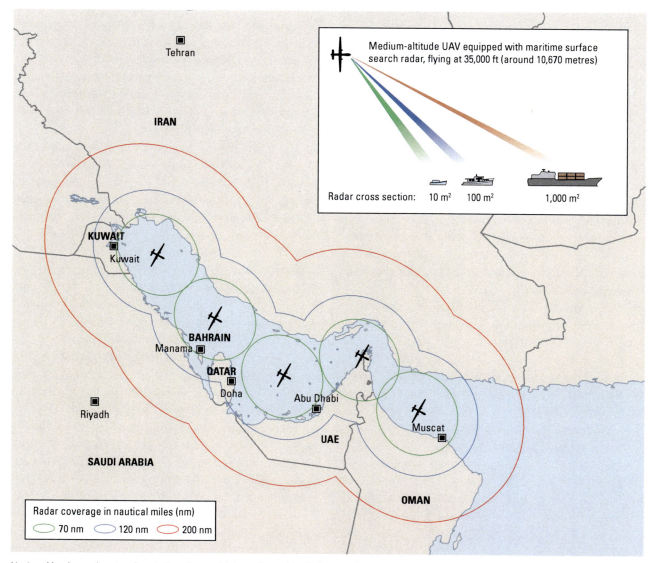

Notional laydown showing five stations from which medium-altitude long-endurance UAVs equipped with surface search radars could provide a near-comprehensive radar picture of the Gulf and its approaches

adding to the difficulties in allocating maritime ISR and other maritime-security assets. Iran's support of its regional partner forces by the maritime route is another factor to be considered in terms of ISR needs.

Compared to the Tanker War in the 1980s, the information space has changed dramatically, both in terms of accessibility to instantaneous but unfiltered information, and in terms of the leverage of information to gain both tactical and strategic advantage. Attitudes to what represents plausible and implausible deniability, in the context of covert grey-zone activities, are also in flux. In this context, the ability to be able to produce quality ISR to support a particular policy position can also become important, as was demonstrated with the June 2019 US video footage during the limpet-mine attacks that supported the US contention of IRGCN involvement.[14]

Efforts at ISR cooperation in the Gulf

Currently, the US is the only actor in the region able to deliver a comprehensive maritime ISR picture. It has also been at the forefront of efforts to create and encourage multinational cooperative maritime-security frameworks among its allies and partners, but although the potential benefits of such frameworks have been widely acknowledged, progress has been relatively modest.

Information-sharing remains a key challenge. Arrangements for information-sharing appear to be on a need-to-know basis or the result of bilateral negotiation on an ad hoc basis, even with close US allies; there is no framework akin to NATO, or even the Five Eyes agreement. In the most sensitive areas, it appears that the US tends to keep the raw data and fine-grain analysis to itself. There is greater transparency with certain partners if required.

International naval cooperation in the region received something of a spur with the expansion of maritime-

Chapter Five

security concerns following the rise of the threat of piracy from Somalia in the 2000s as part of the fallout from the Somali civil war. This prompted from about 2006 the establishment of a number of multinational naval counter-piracy formations, led by the US, the European Union and NATO, as well as a number of other nations operating independently or semi-independently. At times it has included the deployment of various maritime ISR assets, both airborne and at least on one occasion including a submarine carrying out surveillance. There was also significant cooperation with the international maritime industry. But countering Somali piracy is a very different proposition from what may be required in and around the Strait of Hormuz, so while there may be lessons in terms of frameworks and working together, these may be limited.

Foremost among US-led efforts to encourage maritime-security cooperation has been the Combined Maritime Forces (CMF) framework. Under US Navy leadership, this was created in 2001 in the aftermath of the terrorist attacks of 11 September 2001 on the US. It was initially comprised of 12 members and focused on counter-terrorism. It later expanded to 33 nations and was organised into three combined task forces (CTFs): CTF 150, established in 2002, is focused on counter-terrorism operations in international waters in the Middle East and northern Indian Ocean; CTF 151, established in 2009, is the CMF force focused on counter-piracy in the Somali Basin and the Gulf of Aden; and CTF 152, established in 2004, is comprised chiefly of personnel from the Gulf Cooperation Council (GCC) and coordinates maritime security within the Gulf.[15]

Significantly, in order to achieve the widest participation, the CMF focuses on non-state-based threats to maritime security. However, access to any kind of combined ISR picture is very limited. For these reasons, transforming the CMF into something more robust would be a challenge, hence the US pursuit of a different framework in the shape of the International Maritime Security Construct. This was created in response to the incidents in and around the Strait of Hormuz in mid-2019 that were blamed chiefly on Iran.

Another US-led initiative, starting in 2010, has been to bring together a broad coalition of states and ships for the International Mine Countermeasures Exercise (IMCMEX) series. This began very much as an MCM exercise focused on the Strait of Hormuz and the implicit threat from Iran, but has grown into a broader maritime-security exercise (and changed its name to International Maritime Exercise, or IMX) stretching from the Suez Canal and the Red Sea to the Gulf.

Again, the level of ambition in terms of contribution from some participants is modest. In a real MCM scenario, the key contributions will likely come from those actors such as the UK who maintain permanent capabilities in the region and carry out the enduring route survey and pattern-of-life tasking that provide that part of the maritime domain awareness picture.

The other obvious framework for maritime-security cooperation is the GCC. However, while there is clearly an ambition to do more, progress in this area has remained limited. Declared initiatives have included the establishment of a joint GCC maritime-operations centre in Bahrain and the creation of a joint maritime capability under the name Task Force 81, but there has been little tangible action.

Indeed, although it was created in 1981, the GCC has not yet succeeded in becoming a robust and integrated military alliance.[16] The cohesiveness of the GCC has not been helped by the recent antagonism between Qatar and most of the other Gulf states, but a large part of the challenge is the long-standing issue of a lack of standardisation and inter-operability of equipment, making coordination difficult and blunting some of the potential advantages of the quite significant procurement outlays that a number of GCC states have made in respect of their naval forces. Another hurdle remains the continuing reluctance of GCC states to share information with each other, or even internally among their own national force structures.

Another issue is the question of maritime-security priorities, with significant indicators that most GCC states are more interested in the protection of territorial waters and guarding against criminality at sea (such as smuggling) than in, for example, sea control and the protection of SLOCs. A number of GCC states are therefore more inclined to focus on their coastguards than their navies for the provision of maritime security and maritime domain awareness. As a result, these states have invested in significant networks of coastal sensors to help protect port infrastructure. Bahrain has a coastal surveillance system that includes a number of radars and eight long-range FLIR cameras connected to a maritime-operations centre. To a greater or lesser extent, the other GCC states have also invested in coastal sensor networks.[17]

Nevertheless, the GCC states still seem a long way from generating the kinds of capabilities that would be required to be able to produce, and therefore act upon, their own recognised maritime picture. Not the least of these would be more maritime-oriented airborne assets to provide a more consistent picture; more – and more sustained and coordinated – use of surface surveillance; and the ability to join it all up with a consolidated information and analysis hub.

The International Institute for Strategic Studies

GCC naval capabilities

Although Gulf Arab states have for the most part historically focused on coastal defence, in recent years they have begun investing significantly in both recapitalising and expanding their naval forces. Some have plans to expand their power-projection or expeditionary capabilities.[18] This could have implications in terms of increased maritime ISR capability, and also of an increased ISR requirement. Whether the procurements under way are optimal in terms of real capability needs is another matter, and there is also the question of whether the GGC states will be able to operate these new capabilities to their full potential.

Saudi Arabia has by far the largest navy among the GCC states, divided between its Gulf and Red Sea coasts. Its navy includes seven destroyers and frigates as well as more than 30 other patrol and coastal combatants, to which more than 20 can be added from the Border Guard. The procurement programme includes eight new frigates from the US and Spain. However, Saudi Arabia has struggled to make the most of its assets, and to use them as integrated assets in the pursuit of greater maritime domain awareness.

The UAE has a small naval force but is also engaged in a modernisation programme. It has also, as a result of its involvement in the conflict in Yemen, been more forward in its deployment patterns. Perhaps the most remarkable expansion programme under way is that of Qatar. From a combined naval and coastguard numbering 23 small patrol and coastal combatants, it is procuring six frigates and an amphibious assault ship, the latter of which is also being equipped with a powerful radar suite that could allow it to perform as a significant ISR asset, and there has been considerable investment in new coastguard assets as well.

Oman, which is strategically positioned right on the Strait of Hormuz, has a balanced fleet of 15 medium- and small-surface combatants, as well as six amphibious craft and eight logistics and support vessels. In some ways, Oman has the most appropriate force for delivering maritime situational awareness in and around its waters, and appears to use it effectively. The UK had deployed a small detachment of naval helicopters to assist with maritime-picture compilation, but these were withdrawn in April 2019 as Oman has developed its own capability, including the procurement of four C295 maritime-patrol aircraft, currently the only such capability in the GCC.

Kuwait's navy and coastguard between them have over 50 patrol and coastal combatants and are focused chiefly on local maritime security. Bahrain's navy has one frigate, two corvettes and ten other patrol craft while the coastguard has more than 50 small patrol craft. Of the GCC navies, only Saudi Arabia and the UAE have MCM vessels.

One area where the GCC is relatively strong, and which has implications for maritime ISR, is in multi-role naval helicopters, both shipborne and land-based. Between the GCC states, they have some 50 such machines, while Qatar has a dozen of the naval variant of the NH90 on order.

Elements of Qatar's coastguard take part in a public capability display at the inauguration ceremony for a new coastguard base on 14 July 2019

Chapter Five

Iran's naval capabilities

Paradoxically, in view of the handicap under which it has had to function for so long due to sanctions, Iran does show signs in the way it operates at sea of having a degree of maritime domain awareness and the ability to generate its own RMP. It is also in the position of operating essentially two naval forces: the IRGCN, which has responsibility for Iran's maritime security within the Gulf, and the more conventional Islamic Republic of Iran Navy (IRIN), which shares responsibilities with the IRGCN in the Strait of Hormuz and has prime responsibility outside the Gulf.

Through the husbanding of legacy platforms and with some improvisation, Iran seems to have managed to overcome its lack of access to the most advanced capabilities (not least space-based ones, although Iran is likely to be procuring imagery and other sensor output from commercial satellite sources) to create an effective patchwork of maritime ISR capabilities, apparently linked to an effective command-and-control capability.

The legacy elements include three P-3 *Orion* maritime-patrol aircraft and ten SH-3D *Sea King* anti-submarine-warfare helicopters. There are also a number of F-27 transport aircraft that have been used for maritime surveillance, plus other helicopters. Iran also has its own network of coastal radars; some shore-based signals intelligence and observer units, as well as some based on offshore oil platforms; surveillance from IRGCN and IRIN vessels at sea; and some covert use of commercial vessels.

In addition, since at least 2016, Iran has been using unarmed UAVs to track US warships, including aircraft carriers,[19] as well as warships from other nations through the Strait of Hormuz. Iran's sub-surface forces also provide some surveillance capability, albeit of limited reach and endurance.

Iran has amassed a comprehensive and potentially formidable set of asymmetric sea-denial capabilities that represent the chief challenge for other actors' maritime ISR in the region. Iran has a significant inventory of several thousand sea and limpet mines of various descriptions, while the IRGCN has a fleet of fast attack craft and other high-speed craft, specifically the fast inshore attack craft (FIAC), many of which are armed with anti-ship missiles such as the C-701, C-704 and C-802A. Versions of these weapons also equip shore batteries in significant numbers.

The IRGCN has blazed a trail in the development of the FIAC concept, whereby the speed of FIACs is coupled with the massing of large numbers of boats (i.e., a swarming tactic) in coordinated manoeuvres that exploit the FIAC's low radar signature, which makes tracking very difficult. The IRGCN is still recognised as the foremost operator of these platforms. The confined and congested character of the Gulf and the Strait of Hormuz, together with the debilitating effects that the atmospherics can have on a range of sensors, make these waterways in many respects the ideal hunting grounds for FIACs.[20]

Uniquely among Gulf naval forces, Iran has also invested significantly in a submarine force, operating various conventional, coastal and midget submarines. The recent Iranian claim to have successfully launched an anti-ship cruise missile from one of its small *Qadir*-class submarines could also represent a very significant new

An Iranian navy warship takes part in 'National Persian Gulf Day' on 30 April 2019 in the Strait of Hormuz

maritime ISR challenge, although it is unclear if this represents a real operational capability at this stage.[21]

Being able to build a clear picture of all these potential threats is enormously challenging in the circumstances that are likely to be encountered. The complexities involved place a significant premium on being able to defend in depth, if that can be achieved.[22]

Another potential player in this drama at sea is the non-state actor, exemplified most recently by the Houthi rebels with their various forays at sea with missiles, mines and remote explosive-laden craft. As well as the threat that these represent, another factor in the equation is the kind of maritime ISR they potentially employ.

It has been suggested that the Houthis have developed around 30 coast-watcher stations, which they use along with 'spy dhows', UAVs and the maritime radar of docked ships to assist with targeting.[23] The fact that the US Navy responded to the missile attacks by targeting radar installations that the Pentagon said had been used by the rebels suggested another element of their capability.[24] Potentially, the Houthis are the kind of group that might also be likely to leverage the information available through AIS, including port-call details that would allow those onshore to predict the passage times of certain vessels of interest.

Looking ahead

Clearly the GCC states are engaged in maritime ISR, but not in a coordinated way and little of what information is gathered seems to be shared; some member states are not even ready to share where they are deploying their platforms. The building blocks of capability are certainly present, but there are also significant capability shortfalls in key areas that need to be addressed if the GCC states aim to be more self-reliant. There is a declared ambition to be more integrated, but so far that has not overcome the political inertia that exists. As a result, GCC capabilities as a whole remain significantly less than the sum of their parts.

One lesson of recent events has been that the US is less willing than it has been in the past to shoulder most of the maritime-security burden in the Gulf on behalf of allies and partners, but it has also become apparent that for now it remains the only player able to field certain indispensable capabilities, including in terms of ISR. It is not just that the GCC states cannot replace these – nobody else can either. Any GCC initiative to develop its maritime ISR capabilities will need to satisfy the priorities of all parties. The requirement to be able to maintain sea control and freedom of navigation may be at the top end, but the requirement will also have to include basic maritime-security tasking, including counter-smuggling, search and rescue and, increasingly, environmental monitoring. As well as the surface picture, given the likely trajectory of Iranian capabilities, developments will need increasingly to incorporate the sub-surface environment and surrounding coastal areas, as well as the surrounding waterways beyond the Gulf proper and the Strait of Hormuz. Ultimately, the characteristics of the Gulf and Strait of Hormuz as a maritime domain will require a multi-domain approach in order to deal with all the likely emerging threats.

Notes

1   'Cargo Insurers Can Expect up to $65 million in Exposure Value for Gulf of Oman Attack', Russell Group, 14 June 2019, https://www.russell.co.uk/ConnectedRisk/Risk/393/cargo-insurers-can-face-up-to-65-million-in-exposure-value-for-gulf-of-oman-attack.

2   The list can vary slightly, but normally incorporates the straits of Hormuz, Malacca, Bab el-Mandeb and Gibraltar, the Suez and Panama canals, and the great Cape routes around southern Africa and South America.

3   US Energy Information Administration, 'World Oil Transit Chokepoints', 25 July 2017, https://www.eia.gov/beta/international/analysis_includes/special_topics/World_Oil_Transit_Chokepoints/wotc.pdf.

4   Ronald O'Rourke, 'The Tanker War', US Naval Institute Proceedings, vol. 114, no. 1023, May 1988, https://www.usni.org/magazines/proceedings/1988/may/tanker-war.

5   Congressional Research Service, 'U.S.-Iran Tensions and Implications for U.S. Policy', R45795, updated 30 August 2019, https://fas.org/sgp/crs/mideast/R45795.pdf.

6   David Evans, 'Vincennes: A Case Study', US Naval Institute Proceedings, vol. 119, no. 1086, August 1993, https://www.usni.org/magazines/proceedings/1993/august/vincennes-case-study.

7   Robert H. Reid, 'Navy Faces "New Normal" in Persian Gulf: More Iran Provocations', Stars and Stripes, 27 August 2016, https://www.stripes.com/navy-faces-new-normal-in-persian-gulf-more-iran-provocations-1.425837.

8   Megan Eckstein and Sam LaGrone, 'Admiral: Attacks Like Those on USS Mason Will Become More Common', US Naval Institute News, 27 October 2016, https://news.usni.org/2016/10/27/22246.

9   Sydney J. Freedberg, '"Carrier gap" in the Gulf Is a Symptom, Not a Crisis', Breaking Defense, 9 June 2015, https://breakingdefense.com/2015/06/carrier-gap-in-gulf-is-a-symptom-not-a-crisis/.

10 Jonathan Marcus, 'US Sends Aircraft Carrier and Bomber Task Force to "Warn Iran"', BBC News, 6 May 2019, https://www.bbc.co.uk/news/world-us-canada-48173357.

11 Michelle Wiese Bockmann, 'Seized UK Tanker Likely "Spoofed" by Iran', Lloyds List, 16 August 2019, https://lloydslist.

Chapter Five

maritimeintelligence.informa.com/LL1128820/Seized-UK-tanker-likely-spoofed-by-Iran.

12 Richard Scott, 'Change in the Air: Development of Naval UASs', *Jane's Defence Weekly*, 10 May 2017, https://janes.ihs.com/Janes/Display/jdw65652-jdw-2017.

13 Thom Shanker, 'Simple Low-cost Surveillance Drones Provide Advantage for US Military', *New York Times*, 24 January 2013, https://www.nytimes.com/2013/01/25/us/simple-scaneagle-drones-a-boost-for-us-military.html.

14 Frank Gardner, 'Gulf of Oman Attacks: US Video Shows "Iran Removing Mine"', BBC News, 14 June 2019, https://www.bbc.co.uk/news/av/world-us-canada-48633166/gulf-of-oman-tanker-attacks-us-video-shows-iran-removing-mine.

15 See the Combined Maritime Forces website, https://combined-maritimeforces.com/.

16 Anthony H. Cordesman with the assistance of Nicholas Harrington, 'The Arab Gulf States and Iran: Military Spending, Modernization, and the Shifting Military Balance', Center for Strategic and International Studies, 12 December 2018, https://csis-prod.s3.amazonaws.com/s3fs-public/publication/181212_Iran_GCC_Balance.Report.pdf.

17 Edward H. Lundquist, 'Interview with Brigadier Ala Abdulla Seyadi, Commander, Coast Guard Kingdom of Bahrain', Defense Media Network, 28 September 2017, https://www.defensemedianetwork.com/stories/interview-with-brigadier-ala-abdulla-seyadi-commander-coast-guard-kingdom-of-bahrain.

18 Tom Waldwyn, 'Qatar, Saudi Arabia and the UAE: Expanding Naval Horizons?', Military Balance blog, 26 October 2018, https://www.iiss.org/blogs/military-balance/2018/10/qatar-saudi-arabia-uae-naval-horizons.

19 Yeganeh Torbati and Parisa Hafezi, 'Iranian Drone Flew Over US Carrier in 'Unprofessional' Move: US Navy', Reuters, 29 January 2016, https://www.reuters.com/article/us-usa-iran-drone-idUSKCN0V723R.

20 Richard Scott, 'Surviving the Swarm: Navies Eye New Counters to the FIAC Threat', *Jane's Navy International*, 13 February 2014, https://janes.ihs.com/Janes/Display/jni75976-jni-2014.

21 John Miller, 'Iran's New Threat to Ships in the Gulf', IISS, 6 March 2019, https://www.iiss.org/blogs/analysis/2019/03/iran-new-anti-ship-missile-test.

22 For an insight into the perspective on the challenges facing a frigate commanding officer in a potential confrontation situation in the Strait of Hormuz, read Tom Sharpe, 'Chokepoint Charlie – What It's Like to Operate a Warship in the Strait of Hormuz', Save the Royal Navy, 18 July 2019, https://www.savetheroyalnavy.org/chokepoint-charlie-what-its-like-to-operate-a-warship-in-the-strait-of-hormuz/.

23 Michael Knights, 'The Houthi War Machine: From Guerrilla War to State Capture', *CTC Sentinel*, vol. 11, no. 8, September 2018, https://ctc.usma.edu/houthi-war-machine-guerrilla-war-state-capture/.

24 Matthew Rosenberg and Mark Mazzetti, 'US Ship Off Yemen Fires Missiles at Houthi Rebel Sites', *New York Times*, 12 October 2016, https://www.nytimes.com/2016/10/13/world/middleeast/yemen-rebels-missile-warship.html.

Conclusion

This dossier has sought to consider the use and importance of intelligence, surveillance and reconnaissance (ISR) in the Gulf region, and to examine this in the context of the Gulf Cooperation Council's (GCC) own capabilities. The region continues to be challenged by defence and security issues that will need careful attention if they are to be managed successfully. ISR has a fundamental role to play in this: it is critical to effective operations across all domains, above and below the threshold for what would still be collectively recognised as a war.

Like the International Institute for Strategic Studies' (IISS) 2016 study *Missile-Defence Cooperation in the Gulf*, this dossier has found that some within the GCC have individually addressed national needs. The enabling role played by the United States in the provision of ISR capabilities in the region is recognised by the GCC member states, and several have acquired ISR systems or have procurement projects under way to improve national collection capabilities. However, there appears to be little cooperation among Bahrain, Kuwait, Oman, Qatar, Saudi Arabia and the United Arab Emirates (UAE) when it comes to sharing ISR. As the tensions within the GCC have grown since the 2016 dossier,[1] this makes any progress in terms of increased sharing more difficult.

Demand on US ISR

The recognition that the US is the fundamental enabler for ISR in the region needs to be matched by equal awareness that even Washington's resources are limited.[2] There is already a pull from other combatant demands elsewhere in the world for additional ISR resourcing; this most likely will only increase. Part of the answer to address these growing demands may be to draw on some of the ISR resources presently focused on the region. In turn, there

The activities of the People's Liberation Army Navy – seen here on a drill in the East China Sea – including its emergence as a carrier power, is a growing focus of US ISR in the region

Conclusion

may be a need in Washington to further reconsider some of the systems and capabilities to which it has previously refrained from giving GCC states access.

China has become the pacing threat in US military thinking, and the Indo-Pacific theatre – given its scale – has the capacity to absorb a lot of ISR resources. The continuing speed of development of Chinese military systems, and the increasingly capable Chinese armed forces, will only bolster demand for ISR tasking from various elements of the US services and the intelligence community. As the People's Liberation Army Navy grows in confidence in operating further and further from the littoral and its near seas,[3] again this will fuel interest and requests for greater coverage.

Beijing, however, is not the only peer or near-peer rival that Washington faces. An assertive Russia, with an avowedly nationalist foreign policy, is once again a security concern for Europe and NATO. Washington had reduced its presence in Europe over time from the end of the Cold War up until 2013, but the 2014 Russian annexation of Crimea prompted Washington to increase its presence again as a counter to Moscow. In response to a question on shortfalls in 2017, US Army General Curtis M. Scaparrotti, then head of US European Command (EUCOM), told the Senate Armed Services Committee that one of his concerns was 'my intelligence, surveillance and reconnaissance capacity, given that increasing and growing threat of Russia … I need more ISR.'[4] Areas of renewed ISR focus are the Black Sea, eastern Ukraine and the Baltic region. This has resulted in more European activity for the RC-135W, U-2S and RQ-4 aircraft, while a US Air Force (USAF) detachment of the MQ-9 has been established in Eastern Europe,[5] operating from Poland and Romania. USAF General Tod Wolters, who replaced Scaparrotti as EUCOM head, said that the aim of the MQ-9 deployment was to 'improve our understanding of the battle space in the vicinity of Poland, plus the Baltics'.[6]

Regional ambitions

The Saudi-led intervention in Yemen's civil war, and the Emiratis' direct military support for a faction in Libya, are indicative of the two most capable GCC states' growing extroversion and willingness to act independently. However, the Yemen operation has lasted longer and proved more difficult than the GCC countries had hoped.[7] The effect this may yet have on their readiness in future to use military force other than in US-led operations remains to be seen.

The Royal Saudi Air Force and the UAE Air Force operate modern, multi-role combat aircraft, equipped with the current generation of air-to-surface weapons. The war in Yemen, however, is not necessarily the conflict for which these air forces have primarily trained, and the intervention has also shown gaps in ISR capability and the exploitation process that have required US support.

The political difficulties and public criticism of the Yemen intervention among traditional GCC partners – most obviously but far from exclusively the US – may serve to reinforce perceptions that Washington's relationship with the region is changing. In turn, this may lead GCC states to increasingly attempt to sustain more than one strategic partner. Beijing and Moscow may well see this as an opportunity.[8]

A further lesson being offered from the Yemen campaign is that military capability rests less on hardware, and far more on the users' ability to exercise such systems judiciously and effectively. It is a lesson that the Gulf states continue to learn, to a lesser or greater extent, and that perhaps all armed forces need to revisit on occasion.

While Qatar's acquisition of three different multi-role combat aircraft may represent a credible political hedge, it is only the most recent example of a regional acquisition programme that is driven primarily by political need and not military necessity. The delivery of 36 Qatari Dassault *Rafale* aircraft is already under way, and these will be followed starting in 2021 by 36 F-15QAs and in 2022 by 24 *Typhoons*.[9] The Qatari air force has presently one squadron of *Mirage* 2000 fighters, supplemented by a handful of *Alpha Jets* (an armed jet-trainer aircraft). The challenge to accommodate such a rapid expansion is compounded by the requirements of maintaining and supporting three different types of combat aircraft, however capable.

In the context of ISR, within the GCC there is the further issue of fully embracing the processing, exploitation and dissemination elements of the overall cycle, certainly at the national level, and potentially beyond. A repeated concern voiced by many of those interviewed in the production of this dossier was the reticence among the Gulf armed forces to share ISR-derived material at the inter-service level, coupled with even greater reluctance to provide any product beyond national boundaries. Within the limits of classification and national caveats, the US and its close allies and partners have moved some way from a 'need to know' to a 'need to share' mindset, even if the latter remains an imperfect aim. The benefits include maximising the utility of each other's ISR collectors, and also providing a different perspective on the data gathered to help avoid the risk of groupthink. In terms of capability, if not the procurement process, the NATO Alliance Ground Surveillance project is an example of a multinational approach to high-end ISR.[10]

The stresses and tensions within the GCC mean that any collective approach to ISR is today impossible, but

Conclusion

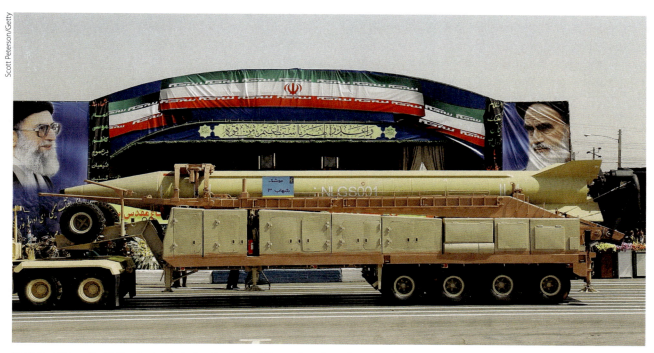

Iran's inventory of ballistic missiles, including the *Shahab*-3, remains a focus for regional concern

there could be opportunities between Saudi Arabia and the UAE that would be mutually beneficial. High-end ISR is expensive and joint procurement could offer cost savings, while resource- and task-sharing would help to get the most benefit out of any investment.

Regional threats and responses

Iran will remain the state of most concern for the GCC, and ought to be a primary requirements driver for ISR and a focus for collection.

A critical element of the threat to the GCC is Tehran's arsenal of ballistic missiles, as explored in *Missile-Defence Cooperation in the Gulf*. Since 2016, Iran has continued to develop its arsenal, with an emphasis on improved accuracy.[11] Of potential worry for the GCC is that this approach could signal a posture more akin to war fighting rather than deterrence, despite Iranian claims.[12] At the same time, Iran has continued to complement the ballistic systems capable of striking the GCC with land-attack cruise missiles. The *Soumar/Meshkat* and *Ya Ali* cruise-missile developments may, as of August 2019, have been joined by a project called *Mobin*, which was shown for the first time at the MAKS 2019 air show held at Zhukovsky near Moscow. The development status of *Mobin* is unknown, but this subsonic design has a claimed range of 450 kilometres. What is clear is that Tehran sees land-attack cruise missiles as a credible support to its ballistic-missile inventory.

Ansarullah, or Houthi, forces in Yemen have also used both ballistic and cruise missiles against Saudi Arabia. Uninhabited aerial vehicles (UAVs) have also been employed as very low-cost guided munitions by the Houthis.[13] The offensive military effect of these is negligible, but their use has considerable propaganda value. Given the size of the territory from which the Houthis can operate, locating and targeting these systems prior to launch presently poses considerable difficulty.

Successful cruise-missile and UAV (used as improvised stand-off munitions) attacks on two Saudi oil installations on 14 September underscored the challenges facing Riyadh in countering such strikes. Saudi government-owned oil company Aramco's Abqaiq processing plant and the Khurais oilfield were the targets of these attacks. The attacks appeared coordinated, with multiple missiles or munitions used against each target. The complexity of the strikes, and the type of cruise missile used, have led the US and Saudi Arabia to allege that the attacks were carried out by Iran rather than the Houthis.

Post-strike analysis of existing ISR information has likely been scoured by the US to try to locate possible launch sites, and perhaps also to identify any training exercises that in retrospect may have been precursors to the attacks. In countering such hostile moves, the Saudi military is faced with multiple challenges, including one of geography. With such a large land mass – mostly uninhabited – and long porous borders, the surveillance demands are considerable. Improvements in ISR, airborne early-warning systems and layered land-based air defence offer a better level of defence, but could never be impenetrable.

Conclusion

Notionally, the most effective way of addressing the ballistic threat is to act prior to the launch of the weapon, a maxim that is also true for the cruise missile. The weapon is at that time a fixed target rather than one re-entering the atmosphere at a high Mach number, or one cruising at subsonic speed at a very low level.

The extent to which any effort achieves the aim of addressing ballistic or cruise missiles prior to their launch is dependent on ISR,[14] since the single greatest challenge is the timely location of the target. Mobile ballistic- and cruise-missile launch systems compound this problem. The capacity to build a picture over time of the deployment and training patterns of threat systems requires space-based ISR, which both Saudi Arabia and the UAE have access to through the use of commercial providers and national technical means. In the event of hostilities, ISR platforms – most of which would be uninhabited – capable of being operated in defended airspace would also be valuable in attempting to track and support the engagement of relocatable systems.

In the Gulf region, the cruise-missile threat extends to the maritime domain. Iran has a substantial inventory of short- and medium-range coastal-defence cruise missiles that are relocatable. Building an intelligence picture of patterns of deployment, training activities and pre-prepared launch sites using ISR collectors is of obvious value in countering such cruise missiles. ISR UAVs have a clear utility in this area, in part because of the persistence of medium-altitude long-endurance UAVs, and in part because of their expendability when compared to a crewed

platform. The loss of a UAV through hostile action does not need to elicit the same response to that of personnel being directly involved in an attack. The same class of UAVs also offers wider utility as an ISR collector contributing to maritime-domain awareness. Given the importance of the Strait of Hormuz, increased capacity in this area would be welcome.

The GCC states will continue to face the challenge of non-state actors; again, the importance of capable ISR in containing and countering such a threat is clear. Border and coastal surveillance and security are concerns for all of the GCC members, and ISR is of importance in addressing these. Given the lengths of some of these borders, persistence is an advantage; employing a mix of crewed and uninhabited platforms is one approach to providing adequate surveillance. Aerostats, in combination with UAVs, would offer a flexible approach to border and coastal surveillance, while not demanding the same level of highly trained aircrew as conventional maritime-patrol aircraft.

Nor should the GCC countries be constrained for choice. Washington is adopting a more liberal attitude to the release of ISR-related systems,[15] particularly UAVs, while China will no doubt try to retain and expand its market share in the region. As with many other behaviours in the Gulf, hedging would appear a likely outcome. In striking deals, however, GCC countries might also want to focus more on the overall production process alongside the collection platform, since in this arena acquisition is easier than exploitation.

Notes

1   'GCC Summit Highlights Tensions with Qatar, Iran', Middle East Policy Council, 13 December 2018, https://mepc.org/commentary/gcc-summit-highlights-tensions-qatar-iran.

2   Tim Ripley, 'Back in the Saddle: Manned Spy Planes Make a Comeback', Jane's Defence Weekly, 13 March 2019, https://janes.ihs.com/Janes/Display/FG_1732168-JDW.

3   US Department of Defense, 'Military and Security Developments Involving the People's Republic of China 2018', 16 May 2018, pp. 8–9, https://media.defense.gov/2018/Aug/16/2001955282/-1/-1/1/2018-CHINA-MILITARY-POWER-REPORT.PDF.

4   C. Todd Lopez, 'Send More Boats, Eucom Commander Tells Senate', US Department of Defense, 5 March 2019, https://www.defense.gov/Newsroom/News/Article/Article/1776402/send-more-boats-eucom-commander-tells-senate/.

5   Kyle Rempfer, 'Air Force MQ-9 Reaper Drones Based in Poland Are Now Fully Operational', Air Force Times, 5 March 2019, https://www.airforcetimes.com/news/your-air-force/2019/03/05/air-force-mq-9-reaper-drones-based-in-poland-are-now-fully-operational/.

6   Tobias Naegele and Brian W. Everstine, 'Wolters on Europe', Air Force Magazine, May 2019, http://www.airforcemag.com/MagazineArchive/Pages/2019/May%202019/Wolters-on-Europe.aspx.

7   Stephen Kalin and Ghaida Ghantous, 'Explainer: Separatist Takeover of Yemen's Aden Leaves Saudi Arabia in a Bind', Reuters, 11 August 2019, https://www.reuters.com/article/us-yemen-security-explainer/explainer-separatist-takeover-of-yemens-aden-leaves-saudi-arabia-in-a-bind-idUSKCN1V10A6.

8   See, for example, Christine Wormuth, 'Russia and China in the Middle East: Implications for the United States in an Era of Strategic Competition', RAND Corporation, Testimony presented before the House Foreign Affairs Subcommittee on Middle East, North Africa and International Terrorism on 9 May 2019, https://www.rand.org/content/dam/rand/pubs/testimonies/CT500/CT511/RAND_CT511.pdf.

9   Tamir Eshel, 'Qatar's Race for Air Power', Defense Update, 11 December 2017, https://defense-update.com/20171211_qatar_air_power.html.

10 NATO, 'Alliance Ground Surveillance', 21 June 2019, https://www.nato.int/cps/en/natolive/topics_48892.htm.

11 'Iran Defends Plan to Improve Missile Accuracy', Deutsche Welle, 29 January 2019, https://www.dw.com/en/iran-defends-plan-to-improve-missile-accuracy/a-47272806.

12 *Ibid.*

13 'Houthis Claim Attack on Military Target in Saudi Capital Riyadh', Al-Jazeera, 26 August 2019, https://www.aljazeera.com/news/2019/08/houthis-claim-attack-military-target-saudi-capital-riyadh-190826111621045.html.

14 US Department of Defense, 'Missile Defense Review 2019', p. viii, 20 January 2019, https://www.defense.gov/Portals/1/Interactive/2018/11-2019-Missile-Defense-Review/The%20 2019%20MDR_Executive%20Summary.pdf.

15 Michael C. Horowitz and Joshua A. Schwartz, 'A New U.S. Export Policy Makes it (Somewhat) Easier to Export Drones', *Washington Post*, 20 April 2018, https://www.washingtonpost.com/news/monkey-cage/wp/2018/04/20/a-new-u-s-policy-makes-it-some-what-easier-to-export-drones/.

Conclusion

Index

Numbers

2K12 *Kub* missile 67
5B satellite 52
9/11 8
9K32 *Strela*-2 missile 67
9K37 *Buk* missile 64
9K317 missile 64

A

A-50U Mainstay aircraft 75
Abu Dhabi (UAE) 70
AC-130 aircraft 74
Aden (Yemen) 32
AeroVironment (US) 17
Afghanistan 8, 12, 16, 17, 34, 35, 36, 55, 61, 62, 63, 64, 65, 66, 74, 80
AGM-114 *Hellfire* missile 66
AH/UH-1 helicopter 42
Airbus (Netherlands) 70
AKD-10 missile 71
al Alawi, Ibrahim Naser 71
Al Dhafra (UAE) 26
Aleppo (Syria) 76
Algeria 70
Alpha Jet aircraft 92
al-Qaeda 6
al-Qaeda in the Arabian Peninsula 67
Alvand-class corvette 42
Aman, Sohail 55
anti-submarine warfare 18, 19
AN/TPS-77 UAV 56
AR-1 missile 52, 53, 54, 70
Arabian Sea 42
Arab Spring 8, 32, 36
AS-15A *Kent* missile 40, 41
Aselsan (Turkey) 52
Ashura missile 40
al-Assad, Bashar 8, 26, 73, 75
Australia 65, 81, 82

B

Bab el-Mandeb Strait 81, 84
BAC *Lightning* 47
BAE Systems (UK) 48, 63
Bahrain 5, 6, 7, 8, 29, 32, 34, 35, 36, 37, 62, 68, 73, 80, 86, 87, 91
  Isa Air Base 62
ballistic missiles 5, 6, 31, 32, 37, 39, 40, 41, 43, 49, 50, 75, 93, 94
Bayraktar TB2 UAV 36, 71
Black Hornet UAV 17
Black Sea 92
Blue Arrow-7 missile 71
Boeing 46, 47, 48, 49, 68, 71
Bombardier (Canada) 66, 69, 71
Broad Area Maritime Surveillance Demonstrator 65, 66
Burraq UAV 54, 55
Bush, George W. 50

C

C-17 heavy transport aircraft 8
C-130 aircraft 55
C-130B *Hercules* aircraft 54, 55
C-130E aircraft 55
C-208 aircraft 53
C295 aircraft 87
C-701 missile 88
C-701/TL-10 *Kosar* missile 41
C-704 missile 41, 88
C-801/YJ-8 missile 41
C-802 *Noor* missile 41
C-802A missile 88
Camp David Accords 64
Canada 49, 65, 84
CH-4A/4B UAV 70, 73
CH-4A UAV 70
CH-4B UAV 53, 70
CH-4 UAV 51, 52, 53, 56
CH-47 *Chinook* helicopter 42
Chieftain tank 42
China 8, 10, 14, 18, 24, 32–34, 37, 38, 40, 41, 45, 48–56, 62, 69, 70, 91, 92, 94
  Chengdu Aircraft Corporation 54
  China Aerospace Science and Technology Corporation 70
  China National Aero-Technology Import & Export Corporation 56
  China Electronics Technology Group Corporation 56
  People's Liberation Army Navy 91, 92
CH-SSC-2 *Silkworm* missile 41
CH-SS-N-4 *Sardine* missile 41
Clausewitz, Carl von 11
Cold War 12, 24, 62, 92
Collins Aerospace (US) 63, 66, 68, 69
Combined Maritime Forces 86
Crimea 92
cruise missiles 5, 6, 37, 40, 41, 42, 43, 49, 50, 51, 80, 88, 93, 94
Cyprus 64
  Akrotiri air base 64

D

Dassault (France) 73, 92
DB-110 system 55, 68, 69, 73
Deptula, David A. 20, 22
Desert Hawk UAV 16, 17

E

E-2 *Hawkeye* aircraft 71
E-2D *Hawkeye* aircraft 83
E-3 *Sentry* aircraft 34, 62
E-7 aircraft 71
Egypt 8, 26, 36, 37, 51, 61, 64, 68, 70, 73
Eleron-3SV UAV 75
EP-3E *Aries* II UAV 62
EQ-4 UAV 66
Erieye UAV 55, 56

ISR & the Gulf: An Assessment

Index

Esper, Mark 62
Ethiopia 37
Eurofighter *Typhoon* 35, 36, 73, 74
European Union 38, 82, 86
exclusive economic zones 18

F

F-4 12
F-14 aircraft 80
F-14 *Tomcat* aircraft 42, 43
F-15 aircraft 36, 37, 68, 69
F-15 *Eagle* aircraft 48
F-15C aircraft 48
F-15QA aircraft 73, 92
F-15SA aircraft 48, 73
F-15S aircraft 48
F-16 aircraft 20, 55, 68, 69, 75
F-16 Block 60 aircraft 8
F-16E/F aircraft 73
F-16IQ aircraft 53
F-22 *Raptor* UAV 34
F-27 aircraft 88
F-35 *Lightning* II 15, 34
F-35B *Lightning* aircraft 83
F/A-18E/F *Super Hornet* aircraft 35, 83
Falcon Eye satellite 70
Falco UAV 54
Farsi Island 82
Fater-1 missile 67
Federally Administered Tribal Areas (Pakistan) 54, 55
First World War 11, 19
Five Eyes agreement 65, 85
Flanker aircraft 42
Forpost UAV 75, 76
France 11, 18, 34, 36, 38, 45, 46, 48, 49
FT-9 bomb 52, 53
Fujairah (UAE) 34

G

G7 49
Gadhafi, Muammar 12
General Atomics (US) 26, 48, 49, 66
Germany 11, 12, 15, 38, 49
Ghader missile 41, 42
Ghadir missile 41, 42
Gibraltar (UK) 82
Global 5000 aircraft 69
Global 6000 aircraft 69, 71, 72, 73
Global Express aircraft 66
GlobalEye UAV 55, 70, 71, 72
Google Earth 55
Granada (Spain) 72
Granat-4 UAV 75, 76
grey zone 6, 14, 15, 31, 80, 84, 85
Gulf Cooperation Council 5–10, 26, 29, 31–37, 39, 41, 43, 45–48, 54, 61, 67, 68, 70, 73, 86, 87, 89, 91–94
  Peninsula Shield Force 7, 8, 36
Gulf of Aden 86
Gulf of Oman 6, 79, 82, 89, 90
Gulf War 13, 31

H

Hadi, Abd Rabbo Mansour 8
Hermes 450 aircraft 17
Hizbullah 64
Hunt, Jeremy 82
Hussein, Saddam 6

I

Ilyushin Il-20 *Coot*-A aircraft 75
India 69
Indian Ocean 86

Indo-Pacific 8, 9, 92
International Institute for Strategic Studies 5, 7, 37, 91
International Maritime Exercise 86
International Maritime Security Construct 86
International Mine Countermeasures Exercise 86
Iran 5–9, 17, 21, 22, 26, 29–43, 61, 64, 65, 73, 74, 79–82, 85, 86, 88, 89, 93, 94
  Islamic Republic of Iran Air Force 42
  Islamic Republic of Iran Navy 42, 80, 81, 82, 88
  Islamic Revolution 38, 80
  Islamic Revolutionary Guard Corps 7, 8, 37, 39, 41, 42, 66
    Basij militia 37, 39
    IRGC navy 42, 81, 82, 85, 88
    Quds Force 37, 39
Iran Air Flight 655 80
Iran–Iraq War 6, 7, 80, 81
Iraq 6, 7, 8, 12, 13, 16, 17, 20, 21, 22, 26, 32, 33, 35, 38, 52, 53, 55, 56, 61, 62, 64, 68, 80, 81, 82
  Air Force 13, 53
  Ba'ath Party 6
Iraq War 13
Islamic State 6, 7, 8, 9, 12, 13, 26, 35, 63, 64, 65
Israel 37, 64, 75, 76
Italy 49

J

Japan 12, 49, 69, 82
JF-17 aircraft 54
Joint Comprehensive Plan of Action 32, 38, 80
Joint Direct Attack Munition 12, 66
Joint Incidents Assessment Team 8, 74
Joint Surveillance Target Attack Radar System 62
Jordan 8, 9, 36, 51, 53, 56, 68, 69, 70, 73

K

Kazakhstan 61
KC-10 aircraft 34
Kh-55 missile 40, 41
Khan, Mujahid Anwar 54
Khashoggi, Jamal 8, 32
Khomeini, Ruhollah 7
Kilo-class submarines 42
King Abdullah (Saudi Arabia) 50
King Air 350 aircraft 69, 73
Kosovo 34
Kosovo War 12, 13
Kuwait 5, 6, 7, 8, 29, 35, 36, 73, 80, 81, 87, 91
  Defense Cooperation Agreement 35
  US bases 35

L

Lebanon 38, 64, 70
Leonardo (Italy) 54, 69, 71
Libya 8, 12, 13, 26, 34, 37, 73, 92
  Libyan National Army 73
Lockheed Martin (US) 15, 17, 26, 54, 56, 62, 68
Long March 2 satellite 52

M

M48 tank 42
M60 tank 42
MAKS 2019 air show 93
Marshall Defence and Aerospace Group (UK) 72
Mecca (Saudi Arabia) 7
Médecins Sans Frontières 74
Mediterranean Sea 19, 76
Merlin helicopter 84
Meshkat missile 41, 93
MiG-25 *Foxbat* 13
MiG-29 *Fulcrum* 37
MiG-31 *Foxhound* 24
MiG-31D aircraft 24

98 The International Institute for Strategic Studies

MiG-31K aircraft 24
Milošević, Slobodan 12
Mirage 2000 aircraft 55, 73, 92
Missile Technology Control Regime 9, 45, 49, 50, 51, 52
Mobin UAV 93
Morocco 8, 70, 73
Moscow (Russia) 93
MQ-1 *Predator* UAV 20, 22, 26, 53
MQ-1 *Predator* A UAV 50
MQ-1C *Gray Eagle* UAV 66, 67
MQ-9 *Reaper* UAV 26, 51, 53, 92, 66, 67, 69, 70
MQ-9 *Reaper/Predator* B UAV 20
MQ-9B *Reaper* UAV 49, 51
MQ-9C *Avenger* UAV 20, 49
Mubarak, Hosni 32

N

Al Nahyan, Mohammed bin Zayed 34, 50
NATO 8, 12, 19, 20, 32, 85, 86, 92
   Alliance Ground Surveillance 92
   Allied Command Transformation 19
   International Security Assistance Force 34
New Zealand 65
Nimrod MR2 aircraft 17
Noor missile 41, 42
Northrop Grumman (US) 26, 49, 62, 63, 65, 71
Norway 79, 82
nuclear-powered ballistic-missile submarine 18

O

Obama, Barack 8
Oman 5, 6, 29, 32, 36, 68, 73, 79, 87, 91
Operation Decisive Storm 32, 35, 36, 73
Operation Desert Storm 62, 81
Operation Earnest Will 80
Operation Enduring Freedom 35, 62
Operation Inherent Resolve 13, 26, 53, 64, 68
Operation Iraqi Freedom 35
Operation Northern Watch 62
Operation Praying Mantis 80
Operation Restoring Hope 64, 73
Operation Sentinel 82
Operation Southern Watch 35, 62
Orlan-10 UAV 75, 76

P

P-3 *Orion* aircraft 69, 88
P-38 *Lightning* 12
Pakistan 45, 50, 54, 55, 56, 68
   Air Force 54, 55, 56
   Armed Forces 54, 55
   M.M. Alam air-force base 54
   Nur Khan base 55
   Operation Barq II 55
   Pakistan Aeronautical Complex 54
   Project Vision 56
Palmyra (Syria) 76
Panama 82
PDV-Mk II missile 24
Persian Gulf 6, 32, 42, 79, 80, 81, 82, 83, 84, 85, 86, 88, 89
Phoenix UAV 17
Pleiades-HR satellite 70
Poland 92
Portsmouth (UK) 82
Putin, Vladimir 24, 43

Q

Qadir-class submarines 88
Qatar 5, 6, 8, 29, 32, 33, 35, 36, 61, 64, 68, 70, 73, 74, 86, 87, 91, 92
   Al Udeid Air Base 61
QinetiQ (UK) 72, 73
Queen Elizabeth-class aircraft carriers 84

R

Raad missile 65
Rafale aircraft 36, 73, 92
RAND (US) 19
Raytheon (US) 63, 66
RC-135 aircraft 62, 64, 65
RC-135U *Combat Sent* aircraft 64
RC-135V/W *Rivet Joint* aircraft 62, 64
RC-135W *Rivet Joint* aircraft 32, 65, 69, 92
RE-3A/B aircraft 64
RE-3 TASS aircraft 69, 73, 74
Reagan, Ronald 47
Reconnaissance Airborne Pod for Tornado 68
Red Sea 32, 81, 84, 86, 87
Revolution in Military Affairs 12
RF-4E aircraft 42
Richardson, John 81
Romania 92
RQ-1 *Predator* UAV 66, 69, 73
RQ-4A Block 10 UAV 22
RQ-4 *Global Hawk* UAV 26, 34, 49, 62, 63, 65, 66, 92
RQ-11 *Raven* UAV 17
RQ-12 *Wasp* UAV 17
RQ-170 *Sentinel* UAV 20, 26
RQ-180 UAV 20
Russia 5, 8, 13, 14, 17–20, 22, 24, 26, 32–34, 38, 41–43, 45, 48, 51, 62, 65, 73–76, 92
   Air Force 75
   Ministry of Defence 75
   Navy 20

S

S-300PMU2 aircraft 43
SA-5 *Gammon* missile 75
SA-6 *Gainful* missile 67
SA-7B *Grail* missile 67
SA-11 *Gadfly* missile 64
SA-17 *Grizzly* missile 64
SA-20 *Gargoyle* aircraft 43
Saab (Sweden) 55, 71
bin Said, Qaboos 36
Sajjil missile 40
Saker 1 UAV 52
Saker 2 UAV 52
Saker 3 UAV 52
bin Salman, Muhammad 33
Sanaa (Yemen) 8, 32
Sat 5A satellite 52
Saudi Arabia 5, 6, 7, 8, 9, 21, 26, 29, 31–37, 41, 45–55, 62, 64, 67–71, 73, 74, 82, 87, 90–94
   Abqaiq processing plant 93
   Al Dhafra Air Base 62, 70
   Al Udeid base 61, 62, 64, 65
   al-Yamamah agreement 47
   Aramco 93
   armed forces 33
   Economic Offset Programme 47
   Khurais oilfield 93
   King Abdulaziz City for Science and Technology 52, 70
   King Faisal Air Academy 52
   King Khalid Air Base 52
   National Guard 33
   Prince Sultan Air Base 69
   Royal Saudi Air Force 8, 47, 48, 52, 64, 68, 69, 71, 73, 75, 74
   Saudi Arabian Military Industries 48
   Saudi Defense Electronics Company 52
   Saudi Technology Development and Investment Company 52
   Space Agency 70
   Tawazun Economic Program 47
   Vision 2030 47, 48, 49
SaudiSat5A/B satellite 70

ISR & the Gulf: An Assessment

Index

Sayyad-2 missile 65
Sayyad-3 missile 65
Sayyad-4 missile 65
ScanEagle UAV 53
Scaparrotti, Curtis M. 62, 92
Sea King helicopter 55, 88
Searcher UAV 76
Second World War 11, 12, 16
   Operation Barbarossa 15
   Operation Market Garden 15
Senegal 8, 73
Shaanxi Y-8G UAV 56
Shaanxi ZDK-03 aircraft 56
Shahpar UAV 54
Sinai (Egypt) 26, 37
Somalia 86
Soumar missile 41, 93
South Africa 45
South China Sea 79
Soviet Union 6, 12, 13, 15, 18, 19, 22, 24, 37, 40, 49, 62, 67, 75, 80
Spain 72, 87
Spitfire PR Mk III 12
SR-71 *Blackbird* aircraft 20
SS-N-30A missile 76
Strait of Hormuz 6, 10, 22, 33, 36, 42, 61, 66, 79, 80, 81, 82, 84, 86, 87, 88, 89, 94
Su-24M2 *Fencer* aircraft 75
Su-24M *Fencer* D 37
Su-30SM aircraft 42
Sudan 8, 37, 70, 73
Suez Canal 86
Suleman, Rao Qamar 55
surface-to-air missiles 13, 22, 65, 67, 69, 72
Swat Valley (Pakistan) 55
Sweden 56, 70, 71, 72, 73
Syria 6, 7, 8, 12, 13, 26, 32, 38, 39, 64, 68, 73, 75, 76, 82
  Army 8
  Hmeimim Air Base 75, 76

T

T-90 tank 42
Takhion UAV 75
Taliban (Afghanistan) 12, 55
Tanker War 6, 80, 85
Thales (France) 69, 70
Tornado aircraft 8, 47, 48, 68, 73
Tornado IDS aircraft 47
TPS 43G UAV 56
transporter erector launchers 5, 6, 21, 39, 40
Trump, Donald 8, 32, 33, 38, 51, 62, 66, 80, 82
Tu-214R aircraft 75
Tupolev (Russia) 75
Turkey 32, 36, 37, 52, 68, 71
  Air Force 75
Typhoon aircraft 8, 37, 48, 92

U

U-2 aircraft 26, 34, 62, 63, 64, 65, 66
U-2 *Dragon Lady* aircraft 62
U-2S aircraft 92
Ukraine 17, 18, 40, 92
Umm Al Melh (Saudi Arabia) 67
uninhabited aerial vehicle 6, 6, 10, 13–22, 24, 26, 32, 34, 36, 37, 42, 45, 48–56, 61, 62, 65–73, 75, 76, 82–85, 88, 89, 93, 94,
United Arab Emirates 5–9, 21, 26, 29, 31–34, 36, 37, 45, 47–52, 54, 55, 62, 64, 66–73, 81, 82, 87, 91, 92, 93, 94
  Air Force 8, 9, 71, 73, 92
  Al Dhafra air base 34, 62, 64, 66, 69, 70
  Economic Vision 2030 47, 48
  Jebel Ali Port 34

Project Dolphin 71, 72, 73
United Kingdom 6, 8, 9, 12, 14–18, 20, 23, 24, 32, 34, 35, 36, 38, 42, 45–49, 55, 64, 65, 69, 72, 73, 74, 80–84, 86, 87
  Air Component Commander 16
  Ajax programme 16
  Army 16, 17
  Cambridge Spy Ring 15
  Carbonite-2 satellite 23
  Long Range Desert Group 16
  Ministry of Defence 20, 23, 82
  Modernising Defence Programme 14
  Multi-National Division (South-East) 17
  Operation Shader 65
  Royal Air Force 64, 65, 68
  Royal Marines 82
  Royal Navy 82, 84, 90
  Royal Regiment of Artillery 17
  Tactical Operational Satellite 23
  Tactical Reconnaissance Armoured Combat Equipment Requirement 16
United Nations 34, 38, 74, 83
  International Maritime Organization 83
  Security Council
    Resolution 1737 38
United States 5–10, 12, 13, 14, 16, 17–26, 29–39, 41, 42, 43, 45–56, 61–67, 69, 70–74, 80–89, 91, 92, 93
  Air Force 22, 23, 26, 34, 61, 62, 64, 65, 66, 67, 74, 92
  Air National Guard 69
  Armed Forces 52
  Army 66, 67
  Central Command 61, 66, 67, 82
  CIA 62
  Combined Air Operations Center 61
  Corona satellite 22
  Defense Intelligence Agency 24
  Department of Defense 12, 24, 25, 51
  European Command 62, 92
  Future Scout and Cavalry System 16
  Grab satellite 22
  KH-8 *Gambit* satellite 22
  KH-9 *Hexagon* satellite 22, 23
  National Air and Space Intelligence Center 23, 24, 39, 40, 41
  National Security Strategy 14
  Navy 10, 22, 62, 64, 65, 80, 81, 82, 83, 84, 86, 89
  Senate Armed Services Committee 92
  State Department 51
UTC Aerospace Systems 68

W

Watchkeeper UAV 17
Westinghouse (US) 56
Wildcat helicopter 84
Wing Loong UAV 51, 52, 54, 71, 73, 74
Wolters, Tod 92
World Trade Organization 46

Y

Ya Ali missile 41, 93
Yemen 5, 8, 9, 21, 26, 29, 31, 32, 34, 35, 36, 38, 41, 52, 64, 67, 73, 74, 75, 81, 87, 92, 74
YLC-2 UAV 56
YLC-6 UAV 56
Yugoslavia 12

Z

al-Zarqawi, Abu Musab 20
ZDK-03 Karakoram Eagle UAV 56
ZDK-03 UAV 56
Zenit-2 satellite 22
Zephyr UAV 20

Made in the USA
Middletown, DE
29 November 2022

16340826R00058